Sport Fish Of New Jersey:
An Angler's Guide

D1548288

Sport Fish Of New Jersey:

An Angler's Guide

By

Manny Luftglass And Ron Bern

With A Foreword By David Chanda,
Director NJ Division Of Fish And Wildlife

Including Coldwater, Warmwater And Marine Introductions
By Jim Sciascia,
Chief Of Information And Education, NJ Division of Fish And Wildlife

Published By:
Gone Fishin' Enterprises

On The Cover. (Top) Here's Manny with a 12 pound dolphin / mahi mahi. (Bottom) Here's Ron with a 5 pound lake trout.

On The Back Cover. (Top fish) fluke. (Middle fish) black crappie. (Bottom fish) hybrid bass.

Sport Fish Of New Jersey: *An Angler's Guide*
By Manny Luftglass and Ron Bern

© 2012 Manny Luftglass and Ron Bern

Published by:
Gone Fishin' Enterprises
PO Box 556, Annandale, NJ 08801
www.gonefishingbooks.com

ISBN: 978-0-9755797-9-4
UPC: 793380 16382-2

Picture Sources: The Authors, New Jersey Division of Fish and Wildlife, Florida Division of Fish and Wildlife, Maine Department of Marine Resources, Diane Rome Peebles provided by the Florida Fish and Wildlife Conservation Commission, Division of Marine Fisheries, Duane Raver, Dave Bosanko, Nick Ferrera and Art Huttemeyer.

Book Design & Typography: TeleSet, Inc., Hillsborough, NJ

PRINTED IN THE UNITED STATES

*This book is dedicated to thousands of people
who help make New Jersey a superb place to fish.
These begin most prominently with the men and women
of the New Jersey Division of Fish and Wildlife,
who creatively manage resources and programs
ranging from trout stocking and fisheries management
to building artificial reefs for fish habitat.
They include many others
in the Department of Environmental Protection
who work tirelessly to maintain the environmental integrity
of our rivers, lakes and bays.
They also include members of dozens of fishing clubs
and conservation organizations, including Knee Deep Club,
Round Valley Trout Association, BassMasters,
Trout Unlimited, Surf Anglers and Muskies Inc.,
to name but a few.*

*This book is dedicated with special appreciation
to those who have helped us in creating
and certifying its contents,
most especially David Chanda,
Director of the Division of Fish and Wildlife,
and Jim Sciascia,
the Division's Chief of Information and Education.
We salute you and we thank you.*

Contents

Sport Fish Of New Jersey:

An Angler's Guide

Here's Director Dave Chanda off the job with a big striped bass.

Foreword

When it comes to fishing opportunities, few other states offer the diversity and quality of both the freshwater and saltwater fishing choices available in New Jersey.

Our state's bountiful freshwater inventory includes over 6,400 miles of rivers and streams and more than 4,000 reservoirs, lakes and ponds larger than one acre. Our freshwater is not only abundant but also incredibly diverse. From the crystal clear glacial lakes and trout streams in the northern counties, to the fertile ponds and reservoirs of central Jersey to the tea-stained acid waters and clear-water sand ponds in southern counties, there's water for every type of angler and every type of fish, which include more than 20 different game fish.

Indeed, freshwater fishing has never been better in New Jersey and books like this are helping spread the word. At no time in our State's history has there been a greater diversity and quality of thriving game fish populations for anglers to pursue. The dramatic improvement in New Jersey's inland fisheries has taken place over the last 30 years through progressive fisheries management and state of the art fish rearing and stocking programs at our Pequest Trout Hatchery and the Hackettstown Warmwater Hatchery. Crowning achievements include the development of a year-round trout fishery and emerging world-class warmwater fisheries for game fish like muskellunge, walleye, northern pike and hybrid striped bass.

On the saltwater front, marine fishery resources are both abundant and diverse with northern species in the winter, southern species in the summer and resident species available year round. New Jersey's vast coastal resources include 127 miles of ocean coastline, 83 miles of bayshore, over 390,000 acres of estuarine area and inlets and easy access to some of the best offshore fisheries in the east bolstered by an ambitious artificial reef program that now encompasses over 25 square miles of sea floor. Our marine resources support the third largest recreational fishery on the United States Atlantic Coast and our marine biologists are working to keep New Jersey in the top three by feverishly navigating the increasingly complex waters of multi-state Atlantic Coast fisheries management.

New Jersey has so many freshwater and saltwater fishing opportunities that it could take a lifetime to sort through them all and experience the best we have to offer. Those of you who have this book have a huge head start by having the most comprehensive guide that exists for learning what is swimming in our waters and where it can be caught in New Jersey. We encourage you to make the time to explore fishing in New Jersey — we're confident you'll be glad you did.

Dave Chanda
Director of the New Jersey Division of Fish and Wildlife

Introduction

From the gin-clear mountain streams to the north to our southernmost deep blue canyons, New Jersey is home to a startling potpourri of sport fish. The angler has but to consider the variety, the size and the splendor of these fish to set the heart racing in anticipation. In fresh water, beautiful shy trout dimple the surfaces of streams and rivers, and big, hungry bass cruise our lakes. Massive muskellunge, northern pike, walleye and pickerel lie in wait in our lakes and rivers for the well cast plug. Offshore, five varieties of tuna, enormous and powerful, swim along the edges of the continental shelf, and blue and white marlin and massive sharks prowl the depths. Closer in, bluefish, striped bass, bonito, dolphin, drum and tautog are but a few of the saltwater species that crowd our salt and brackish waters.

More than one million anglers ply the waters of the Garden State each year with varying degrees of success. Some, it seems, are inevitably luckier than others. But in fishing, as in life, luck is what happens when preparation meets opportunity. The anglers who are most successful are almost inevitably the ones best prepared. They are the ones with the uncanny knack of identifying every species of fish. They know where to fish for them, how to fish for them, when to fish for them. They understand the best tackle to use that day for that fish, the best bait, the most effective presentation. They know how large the fish get to be and they usually have a pretty good idea of how to clean and cook the most delectable species.

`It is with this in mind that we have written this angler's guide to sport fish of New Jersey. We believe it will be extremely interesting and helpful to all anglers, from the first time worm dunker to the most skilled dry fly caster. And we believe that if taken to heart, its useful and easily applied content will help spread the luck around to all.

Ron Bern
Manny Luftglass

New Jersey's
Coldwater Fishery

Quintessential trout streams that tumble and roll through the northern third of the Garden State are a classic fly rodder's dream. The legendary Flatbrook River drainage provides miles of fast riffles and runs over classic rock stretches and deep, silt-bottomed holes where fine trout hold in the shadows. Further south, there is the South Branch of the Raritan River that flows through Ken Lockwood Gorge — a superb two and a half mile stretch of trout habitat whose rushing waters and clear, deep pools are open only to artificial baits. The Pequest offers its own classic trout water, as do the Paulinskill, Musconetcong and Black Rivers and numerous northern tributary streams, and further south, the Manasquan, Metedeconk, Toms, Cohansey and Maurice Rivers.

Some of these are designated wild trout streams, meaning they have their own naturally reproducing populations of trout, mostly brook trout and/or browns.

But flowing water is only half the story of trout fishing in New

Jersey. Lake fishing is an entirely different, but no less satisfying experience. Trout grow faster and larger in large, deep lakes that provide year round temperature and oxygen sufficient to support trout and that contain stocks of forage fish. Indeed, two of the four state record trout were taken in Round Valley Reservoir, a 21 pound 6 ounce brown and a 32 pound 8 ounce laker, and Lake Hopatcong produced the third, a 13 pound rainbow. Along with Merrill Creek Reservoir, Round Valley is designated a trophy trout lake, and with very good reason.

The great trout fishery in New Jersey is a testament to the creative scientific management of the state's freshwater fishery by the New Jersey Division of Fish and Wildlife. As early as 1879, the Division stocked imported brook trout when the native population was thought to have been decimated by a drought. In 1912, the state constructed the Hackettstown Hatchery and began producing catchable brook, brown and rainbow trout. By 1932, Hackettstown was raising over 500,000 trout for distribution throughout the state. In 1980, the Pequest Hatchery was built and soon began raising even larger numbers of catchable trout annually for stocking in 180 lakes and streams. Hackettstown then changed its focus to raising over 2 million warmwater fish each year.

Clearly trout fishing already is a remarkable success story in the Garden State. But the scientists and planners at the NJ Division of Fish and Wildlife are not content to rest on their laurels. Seeing an opportunity to develop a new and exciting sport fishery, the state is experimenting with a sea-run brown trout program in the Manasquan River. To date, some 250,000 browns have been stocked in the tidal portion of the river. In 2006, the Division began introducing another salmonid, the landlocked salmon, into Wawayanda Lake and Aeroflex

Lake, both of which have sufficient size and depth and the required forage base to support a salmon population.

Bottom line? There is a fantastic coldwater fishing experience awaiting dry fly enthusiast and live bait angler alike, right around the corner.

Jim Sciascia
Chief of Information and Education
New Jersey Division of Fish & Wildlife

Jim Sciascia with a very nice brown trout.

Trout, Brook

Noted fishing writer Lee Wulff once observed, "A game fish is too valuable to be caught only once." This wisdom especially comes to mind when an angler lands a brook trout. Quite possibly the most beautiful of all fresh water species, the brookie is the only salmonid native to New Jersey and has been designated the state fish.

DESCRIPTION: Brook trout are actually members of the char family and on average are smaller than brown or rainbow trout. Gray to olive green on the back, brook trout have wormlike markings on the back and dorsal fin and an identifying white stripe on each lower fin. The sides are lighter in color with bluish halos around pink or red spots and brilliant orange stripes down each lower side.

WHERE AND WHEN: Naturally reproducing brook trout populations, mostly found in streams in the northern part of the state, have been augmented over many years by the state. Brookies were the first fish raised and stocked by the state when in 1913, 86,700 fingerlings were transported from the new Hackettstown Hatchery to a number of New Jersey streams. The fish travelled in milk cans packed in ice in the back of a chain-driven REO truck. Brook trout need richly oxygenated water, generally at temperatures of 53 degrees or colder. Because of this, brookies actively migrate up and down rivers and streams all year looking for the right conditions. Brookies are generally found in the headwater sections of rivers and

around cold tributary streams. There are known to be no less that 123 streams containing naturally reproducing brook trout in the state, including Bear Swamp Creek, a feeder stream to the Ramapo River, and the upper sections of the Saddle River. This is especially significant since spawning trout are sure indictors of clean, healthy waters. Anglers need to be aware of seasonal closings, including weeks when fish are stocked.

BAIT AND TACKLE: Fishing for brook trout is often thought to be exclusively an exercise in flycasting, and certainly many fall to the well presented fly. The best daytime fishing is done with nymphs throughout the pockets and streamers in high water conditions. These handsome fish are omnivorous feeders and also can be taken on salmon eggs, worms, natural insects and small spinners.

STATE RECORD: It has been said of the generally smaller brookie that a 12 inch fish is a virtual trophy. However, the state record brook trout, caught in the Rockaway River by angler Andrew DuJack in 1995, tipped the scales at 7 pounds 3 ounces.

FOOD VALUE: The brook trout has a delicious flavor, with flaky meat ranging in color from white to pinkish-orange. ■

Trout, Brown

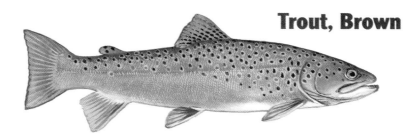

The brown trout is said to be the perfect freshwater game fish and with good reason. Browns grow faster, live longer and attain greater size than brook trout or rainbows. They thrive in habitats that are inhospitable to other trout. Most important, they are by nature night feeders and among the wariest of fish, such that the fine brown that succumbs to a perfectly presented fly is a singular achievement.

IDENTIFICATION: The brown trout is golden to olive brown on back and sides, with large dark spots and smaller red spots lightly haloed on sides and fins. The brown is distinguished from its close relative, the landlocked salmon, by its square tail. Young browns feed on insects and other invertebrates, while larger fish morph into predators of other fish and whatever insect life is available and abundant.

WHERE AND WHEN: The perfect habitat for browns is clear, cool to cold water in streams, rivers and lakes, with rocky substrate and an abundance of cover. The state introduced the first browns into New Jersey waters more than 100 years ago and exceptionally well managed stocking programs over the intervening years have led to naturally reproducing populations in 76 streams in the Northern half of the state. A recent statewide stocking included 163,000 browns averaging just under 11 inches in length, with another 2,215 from brood stock ranging from 16 to 21 inches. The state's free flowing rivers provide fine habitat for browns, prominently to include the Big Flatbrook, with its prolific hatches of light cahills, blue winged olives, sulphurs and March browns, and the South Branch of the Raritan, with its outstanding hatches of hendricksons, blue quills, little yellow stoneflies, cahills and gray caddis. Stream anglers should look for quiet water with plenty of cover. Brush piles, rock shelves, logs and cutbanks are favorite haunts of big brown trout.

A sea run brown trout fishery has been established with stocking programs in the tidal section of the Manasquan River. Some stocked trout move upstream to freshwater while others move downstream and out to sea where they may remain for years before returning in an attempt to spawn. The sea runs are elusive and present a superb angling challenge.

BAIT AND TACKLE: Angling for brown trout is often thought of in context with fly rods, wet or dry flies and gently flowing streams. In fact, browns are caught in a variety of habitats (prominently to include Merrill Creek Reservoir and Round Valley Reservoir, New Jersey's Trophy Trout Lakes) with spinning tackle and various natural baits and artificials.

STATE RECORD: The state record brown trout weighed 21 pounds 6 ounces and was caught in the Valley of the Giants (Round Valley Reservoir) in 1995 by Lenny Saccente.

FOOD VALUE: Like the rainbow and brookie, the brown is wonderful table fare, with fine delicate flavor that requires little culinary enhancement. ■

Trout, Lake

The lake trout is by a considerable margin the largest salmonid species to be found in New Jersey. Indeed huge lakers have principally buttressed Round Valley Reservoir's reputation as "The Valley of the Giants."

DESCRIPTION: Lakers have the typical trout shaped body covered with light spots on a darker background of green or grayish brown and a deeply forked tail. They require cold, oxygen-rich waters and feed on the most abundant food sources. Some adult fish seem to prefer so-called planktivorous diets such as tiny shrimp-like creatures (gammarus) found at bottom in deep water while others prefer a piscivorous diet of herring and shiners. The lakers that feed principally on fish grow faster and mature at a larger size.

WHERE AND WHEN: Introduced into Round Valley in 1977, the lake trout thrived in the deep clear waters of the reservoir and soon established a naturally reproducing population. Of note: this is thought to be the most southern range for lakers' natural reproduction in the country. Indeed, lake trout reproduction in Round Valley has been so successful that bag limits have been increased in the interest of fishery management. A thriving population also has been established in Merrill Creek Reservoir, a second excellent venue for laker fishing, and stocking programs have begun in Monksville Reservoir.

In early Spring, lakers can be found throughout the entire water column. However,

as surface temperatures increase, lakers seek deeper, cooler waters near bottom, increasingly relating to bottom. Of note: lake trout are regulated by seasonal and size/bag limits.

BAIT AND TACKLE: Deepwater trollers utilizing downriggers and spoons or crankbaits are especially successful in the summer months. Bait fishing with herring or large shiners and jigging at or near bottom in deeper water also account for splendid catches. The angler should exercise care in retrieving fish from deep water, since too fast a retrieve will result in a fish that may die from "the bends."

STATE RECORD: The sheer size of the largest lake trout makes them an especially exciting quarry. The state record laker is a 32 pound 8 ounce monster caught in 2002 in Round Valley Reservoir by Greg Young. It is likely that still larger lakers prowl "The Valley's" depths, since the world record lake trout weighed more than 100 pounds. Indeed, a fish somewhat larger than the record was caught in the 2011 net sampling by the state and released unharmed.

FOOD VALUE: Lakers are fine table fare, with delicate flesh that deserves special care in preparation. ■

Trout, Rainbow

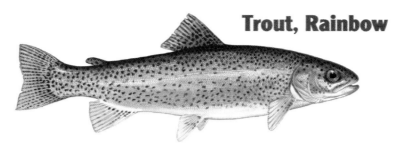

A noted outdoor writer once observed that "Pound for pound, the rainbow trout is the most beautiful, tenacious and acrobatic creature in the sportsman's bag." It is possible that brook trout enthusiasts might argue beauty, and hybrid bass anglers will certainly contest tenacity. But the "bow" is nonetheless the stuff of angler's dreams, most especially the stream angler who envisions a fine two pound fish rising up from a moss covered stream bottom to take his (or her) perfectly presented dry fly.

DESCRIPTION: The rainbow is the most recognizable of freshwater game fish due to the pink to red stripe running lengthwise along its sides. Its body is salmon-shaped and heavily speckled, with an olive colored back shading to silvery white undersides.

The rainbow is one of the special gifts of the State Division of Fish & Wildlife to the anglers of New Jersey. Each spring, the Division stocks no less than 100 streams and 80 lakes across all of the state's 21 counties with upwards of 600,000 trout, averaging 10.5 inches and ½ pound in size. In the fall, an additional 20,000 trout, measuring 14 to 16 inches are stocked in 30 carefully selected streams, lakes and ponds plus 1,000 rainbow breeders averaging 20 inches. In winter, another stocking of large trout occurs.

WHERE AND WHEN: To spawn and hold over, rainbows require cool, well oxygenated water such as the fine trout streams that tumble through the northern third of the state. The Big Flatbrook is one of the state's classic trout venues, as are the Little Flatbrook and the portion of the South Branch that flows through Ken Lockwood Gorge. There is an especially abundant supply of rainbows in the Paulinskill, where nymph fishing is very productive in some of the faster pocketed stretches. However, fishing for rainbow trout is a statewide affair, with trout taken in a wide variety of styles and tackle suited to the venue. Consequently, whereas the flyrod and wet fly are suited to the fast riffles and silt-covered holes of the Flatbrook, the spinning rod is much more often brought into play in fishing the crystal waters of Round Valley Reservoir, the quietly flowing waters of the Musconetcong River or any of the 80 ponds and lakes in which trout are stocked.

BAIT AND TACKLE: "Bows" are not the epicures they often are made out to be. Young trout eat aquatic insects like caddis flies and midges, and as they grow larger, they add small fish and larvae to the menu. Adult trout, however, are attracted to a surprising variety of baits such as shiners, alewife herring, glass worms and baby night crawlers.

STATE RECORD: The state record rainbow, weighing an even 13 pounds, was caught in 1988 in Lake Hopatcong, the state's largest lake, by Gene Rutkowski.

FOOD VALUE: The rainbow trout is highly prized for its delicate flavor. ■

Salmon, Landlocked

Salmon, often referred to as the king of freshwater fishes, is the newest addition to the superb sport fishery in New Jersey. In 2006, the NJ Division of Fish and Wildlife re-introduced landlocked salmon into Lake Aeroflex and Wawayanda Lake, both of which are deep enough to provide sufficiently cold water and enough dissolved oxygen to sustain life year-round. Salmon were originally stocked in New Jersey waters more than 50 years ago but the practice was suspended for decades. In a recent stocking, 1,500 salmon averaging just over 8 inches in length were float stocked in Wawayanda and another 500 in Lake Aeroflex, continuing the state's commitment to establishing an exciting new fishery.

DESCRIPTION: Landlocked salmon trace their lineage back to the Ice Age, when sea-run populations were trapped in lakes by receding runoff streams. Identification is important, since salmon share waters with brown trout, a close relative. The salmon is generally silvery in color, often with small x-shaped markings on the back and sides. The surest means for differentiating salmon from brown trout is the tail: the salmon's tail is forked while the brown's tail is square.

WHERE AND WHEN: As noted, the state has established fisheries in Lake Aeroflex and Wawayanda Lake. Early spring and late fall are ideal fishing periods; however, many fish are taken right after ice-out. In summer, salmon anglers drift or suspend spinners, jigs and live baitfish fairly deep in the water column.

BAIT AND TACKLE: One handed spinning tackle is appropriate to the task of catching salmon, usually with 8 to 10 pound test line. A favorite approach is trolling lures like the Phoebe or live baitfish at a predetermined depth in the water column, usually with the use of downriggers. Salmon also are occasionally caught by slow trolling live bait and lures near the surface in cold weather.

STATE RECORD: The state record landlocked salmon clearly reflects the state's early stocking programs. In 1951, an angler named John Mount took an 8 pound salmon in Lake Aeroflex (formerly New Wawayanda) that still stands as New Jersey's record.

FOOD VALUE: The landlocked salmon is one of the most delicious of all the salmonids. (Note: regulations should be carefully checked, since catch and release may be in order in some venues.) ■

New Jersey's
Warmwater Fishery

From the crystal clear glacial lakes in our northern counties to the fertile ponds and reservoirs of Central Jersey to the tea-stained waters in southern counties to 6,400 miles of free flowing rivers and streams, the fishing opportunities for warm water fish are beyond exceptional. It is a truism that the fishing has never been better in New Jersey.

The size and variety of species in our small and heavily populated state is remarkable. Powerful muskellunge cruise the channels of the upper Delaware River as well as Greenwood Lake, Monksville Reservoir, Echo Lake Reservoir, Mountain Lake and Lake Hopatcong. Hefty walleye provide wonderful year round fishing in Swartswood Lake, Canistear Reservoir, Greenwood Lake and Lake Hopatcong. Largemouth bass thrive in most of the state's still waters and smallmouths terrorize forage fish in cool, clear streams and deep, clear lakes like Wanaque Reservoir, Monksville Reservoir, Clinton Reservoir, Spruce Run Reservoir, Echo Lake, Greenwood Lake, Round Valley Reservoir and Lake Audrey. Hybrid striped bass, the fastest and most powerful of fresh water fish, create long, heart-stopping runs every time they take a bait in Spruce Run Reservoir, Lake Hopatcong and the Manasquan Reservoir. Massive channel catfish, often weighing in double digits, prowl the Delaware and Maurice Rivers and major bodies of still water like Assunpink, Mary Elmer and Sunset Lakes. Scrappy panfish by the millions, including yellow perch, sunfish, black crappie, white crappie and rock bass, populate waters throughout the state and account for nearly half of the total freshwater fish harvest.

A number of factors combine to make New Jersey a great fishing destination. The Clean Water Act of 1972 has improved water quality dramatically. The creation of new reservoirs and increased public access to state waters are other factors, as is the increasing popularity of catch and release. However, the most significant is the state's intensive management of existing fisheries and introductions of new species. Over the past three decades, for example, the Division of Fish and Wildlife's Bureau of Freshwater Fisheries has implemented bold and ambitious programs that brought us muskellunge, northern pike, walleye and hybrid bass, in addition to smallmouth and largemouth bass, tiger muskies channel catfish and other species over longer periods of time. It is notable that only seven of the 38 freshwater species featured in this Guide are native to New Jersey — chain pickerel, brook trout, pumpkinseed and redbreast sunfish, American eels, white catfish and bullheads. All of the remaining 31 species have been introduced into New Jersey's waters in stocking programs over more than 100 years.

It is no accident that fishing in the Garden State is superb.

Jim Sciascia
Chief of Information and Education
New Jersey Division of Fish & Wildlife

Bass, Largemouth

The largemouth bass is the most pugnacious and avidly sought game fish in the Garden State. Nationally televised bass fishing tournaments reflect the public's enthusiasm for bass. The hard, slashing strike of the largemouth and its acrobatics once hooked explain its popularity with serious anglers.

DESCRIPTION: The largemouth is easy to distinguish from its close relative, the smallmouth bass. As its name implies, the former has an exceptionally big mouth, with the hinge of the jaw extending past the rear of the eye. The largemouth is basically dark green on the back that fades to white on the belly, usually with a dark lateral line. The color varies with changes in environment and spawning activity.

WHERE AND WHEN: The largemouth is found in virtually every lake, pond, slow moving river or stream from the northernmost counties south to Lake Lenape at Mays Landing. Despite its widespread distribution, the largemouth is not native to New Jersey. It was first stocked in Jersey waters over a century ago. This effort continues today as fingerlings are stocked in scores of ponds (e.g., Bests Pond, Shaws Mill Pond, Pomphrey Pond) and lakes (Mirror Lake, Lake of the Lillies, Spruce Run Reservoir) each year. Like a lot of predator fish, largemouth bass tend to be more active early and late in the day due to changes in light intensity. For the same reason, bass are more likely to feed on cloudy days than so-called bluebird days. In the warmer months, successful bass anglers concentrate on structure such as weed beds, fallen trees, docks and brush piles. Anglers fishing deeper waters work bait or lures around points, offshore humps, wood piles and drop-offs.

BAIT AND TACKLE: Entire sections of sporting goods stores and tackle shops are devoted to an incredible array of crankbaits, jerkbaits, stickbaits, topwater lures, plastic worms, jigs and spinner baits thought to be attractive to bass. And when the mood is upon him, old "bucketmouth" will strike any one of them, along with an array of natural foods ranging from fish and crayfish to baby ducklings. It is thought that the largemouth is the most intelligent freshwater fish, able to distinguish and avoid a particular type of lure after only one encounter with it. This may help determine strategy for aficionados working the weedy bays and points in New Jersey's lakes and ponds. Note: the closed season on bass is April 15 through June 15 every year.

STATE RECORD: The state record largemouth was a 10 pound 14 ounce leviathan caught in 1980 in Menantico Sand Wash Pond by angler Robert Eisele.

FOOD VALUE: The largemouth is the centerpiece of many a fine dinner. ◾

Bass, Rock

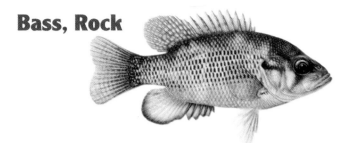

It has been said that rock bass are more often caught than sought, and with good reason. The scrappy little pan fish occupies habitat that is ideal for smallmouth bass and crappie and readily takes shiners that are intended for larger game fish.

DESCRIPTION: Rock bass are easy to identify, primarily because of very large mouths and red eyes. They range from light silver color with rows of dark spots to dark bronze with brassy yellow flecks and dark brown saddles along the sides. They have the ability to change from dark color to light, depending upon habitat, and this helps account for their significant survival rates.

WHERE AND WHEN: Rock bass prefer clear streams, rivers and lakes with a rocky bottom and they often hide out of the current near boulders, rock piles or tree roots. Mature fish reach lengths of six to ten inches and feed on small fish and crayfish.

BAIT AND TACKLE: Because they are schooling fish, rock bass are easy to catch once located. Catching rock bass is great fun for youngsters new to rod and reel, especially since the action is often quite fast. Rock bass take minnows, worms, grubs and small pieces of cut bait, presented on a small hook and light line, generally under a bobber. Almost any tackle will suffice.

STATE RECORD: Weighing one pound 5 ounces, the state record rock bass was caught in the Saddle River by Eric Avogardo in 1982.

FOOD VALUE: With the exception of Eric's record fish and perhaps a few others, rock bass are generally too small and bony to have much appeal as table fare. ▧

Bass, Smallmouth

The smallmouth bass is pound for pound one of the hardest fighters of all freshwater sport fish, often thought to be second only to the hybrid bass in power and tenacity. Its surging runs and acrobatic leaps make the "smallie" a great favorite among knowledgeable Garden State anglers.

IDENTIFICATION: Distinguishing smallmouths from their largemouth cousins relies most significantly on placement of the jaw. In the smallmouth, the hinge of the jaw never extends as far back as the eye. Its color varies with habitat, ranging from green to brownish copper (the latter explaining nicknames like "bronzeback" and "bronze bass.")

WHERE AND WHEN: Smallmouths are another gift to anglers from the state, with earliest stockings beginning in the late 1800s. "Smallies" generally prefer large, clear-water lakes and cool clear streams with moderate current; therefore the state's stocking programs concentrate on major lakes. In a recent stocking, 21,513 fingerlings were released in six lakes: Lake Audrey, Union Lake, Manasquan Reservoir, Spruce Run Reservoir, Tilcon Lake and Split Rock Reservoir. Healthy populations of smallmouth also can be found in a variety of moving waters, up to and including the mid and upper reaches of the Delaware River. As with the largemouth, the long-standing closed season on smallies is April 15 through June 15.

BAIT AND TACKLE: Smallmouths prey on crayfish, hellgrammites, small fish and insects and are often caught on natural baits, as well as jigs, soft plastic stickbaits and other artificials which imitate naturals. Anglers are most successful from spring through late fall, when smallies begin to school up and feed heavily. Light spinning tackle and bait casting outfits generally are employed, and live baits, including shiners, alewife herring and nightcrawlers, produce good catches.

STATE RECORD: The state record smallmouth was caught in Round Valley Reservoir in 1990 by angler Carol Marciniak. It tipped the scales at 7 pounds 2 ounces.

FOOD VALUE: The "smallie" is superior table fare, its white flesh succulent and firm. ▦

Bluegills

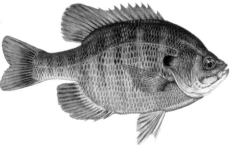

It has been said that if you catch a 12 oz. bluegill, you will swear it weighs a pound. This is because of the unparalleled scrappiness of this exceptionally useful fish.

DESCRIPTION: The bluegill is slab sided with a small mouth and a dark blue to black rounded gill flap from which it derives its name. It has five to nine dark bars on its side and generally is an overall dark green color, although this can change with water clarity and spawning phase.

WHERE AND WHEN: The bluegill may be the most widely distributed fish in the state; indeed, it is thought that virtually everyone in New Jersey lives no more than five minutes from a fishable population. Moreover, because of their schooling habits, their abundance, their aggressiveness and the ease with which they are caught, the entire panfish community and most especially the bluegill is the perfect introduction of the young angler to a lifetime love of fishing.

Bluegills, like pumpkinseed and redbreast sunfish, are prolific spawners and repopulate waters as fast as they are harvested. Nonetheless the state still raises and stocks bluegills in selected ponds and lakes, not least because they are in the middle of the food chain. Farrington, Ramapo, Ryker and Maple Lakes are known to have fine bluegill populations, while thousands more are stocked in venues such as Lake Nelson, Heritage Park Pond, Lake of the Lillies and Scout Lake.

BAIT AND TACKLE: Bluegills can be caught throughout the year, although the months of May to October are the most productive. A simple small hook, split shot and bobber arrangement fished with a worm at depths of two to eight feet is usually all that is required. Like yellow perch and pike, bluegills can readily be caught through the ice, usually by jigging small spoons or small jigs tipped with meal worms or grubs. Light spinning tackle, fly rods and even the classic cane pole are ideal equipment for bluegills.

STATE RECORD: The state record bluegill weighed in at an even three pounds. It was caught by angler Dom Santarelli in a private farm pond in Pennington.

FOOD VALUE: Although generally small, the bluegill is more than worth the trouble to clean and prepare, given its superb quality as table fare. ▪

Bowfin

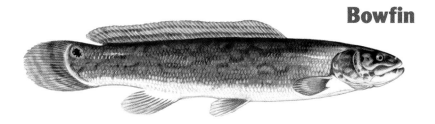

The bowfin is a throwback to Jurassic and Eocene eras. Fossil remains show three additional species of bowfin existed 250 million years ago, but only the primitive ray-finned creature we encounter today in New Jersey ponds and creeks has survived over the centuries.

DESCRIPTION: Bowfin are easily identified by their long dorsal fins running from mid-back to the base of the tail. They are able to breathe air, utilizing swim bladders as a primitive lung, and can be seen coming to the surface and gulping air. They are voracious and largely indiscriminate feeders, ambushing or stalking fish, frogs, insects and crawfish.

WHERE AND WHEN: Bowfin are found in a wide variety of shallow, weedy lakes, ponds and backwaters of streams, including White City Lake, Mullica Hill Pond, Hainsville Pond, Pepaupo Creek, Gibbstown Floodgates, Spring Lake, Raccoon Creek, Oldmans Creek and the Delaware River. They occasionally rise to artificial lures but more often strike on live or cut bait. One angler even reported excellent success with bits of beef heart. A small but dedicated band of bowfin anglers has sprung up in New Jersey. They claim a bowfin will strike as hard as a bass, put up an extremely tough fight and grow as large as 20 lbs.

STATE RECORD: The state record bowfin, although large, does not bear out the claim of 20 lb. monsters. The record fish, caught in the Delaware River in 2011 by angler Chris Hoffman, weighed 10 pounds 14 ounces.

FOOD VALUE: Bowfin are not normally recommended for the table, not least because these fish accumulate higher levels of mercury in their tissue than most fish do. The state recommends that bowfin be released unharmed. ▩

Bullhead, Brown

The brown bullhead, a native to New Jersey, is a most accommodating fish to anglers. It resides in generally accessible waters and it is tolerant of warm temperatures and low oxygen levels that would kill other fish. Perhaps best of all, it is easy to catch. Thus, like sunfish, brown bullheads are perfect first targets for junior anglers more interested in action than quality.

DESCRIPTION: Brown bullheads are identified by their scaleless skin (generally dark brown in color), mottled sides, thick bodies and distinctive barbels. Occasionally brown bullheads are more yellow than brown. They are opportunistic bottom feeders, eating fish, worms, snails, crayfish and aquatic vegetation.

WHERE AND WHEN: Bullheads thrive in a variety of habitats but do especially well in ponds and lakes with soft mud bottoms and plenty of vegetation. Although they are naturally occurring, the state still stocks small numbers of fish in 40 or so ponds and small lakes each year to generate additional breeding populations. Most stocked fish are 10 to 15 inches long. Verona Park Pond, Roosevelt Park Pond, East Brunswick Park Pond and Black Brook Park Pond are typical stocked venues.

BAIT AND TACKLE: Fishing for bullheads is an exercise in bottom fishing, with night crawlers, cut fish, liver or corn as bait on a #4 or #6 hook held stationary by a small egg sinker. Chumming with bits of cut bait or canned corn will speed the action.

STATE RECORD: Brown bullheads are generally smaller than other catfish species. The state record fish, caught at Lake of Woods/Fort Dix by Gary Schmidt in 1997, tipped the scales at 4 pounds 8 ounces.

FOOD VALUE: Epicures may pass on bullheads but in actual fact their red meat is quite tasty, especially when rolled in cornmeal and deep fried. ■

Carp, Common

The common carp is anything but common. Indeed, it is the most under-appreciated sport fish among Garden State anglers. The power and tenacity of its fight are comparable only to the Hybrid Bass among fresh water fishes, and its size is second to none. In many other countries, carp fishing has evolved into a sport with as much popularity as bass fishing here in the United States. In the United Kingdom, the carp is the most sought after game fish species. Izaak Walton, the prototypical 17th Century British angler, wrote about carp in *The Compleat Angler*, "The carp is the queen of rivers; a stately, a good, and a very subtil (sic) fish."

DESCRIPTION: Carp are copper to bronze in color, with large, thick scales and one dorsal fin containing 15 to 19 spines. Native to Asia, carp were first stocked as a food fish in the United States in the 1870s and were spread by state governments to most U.S. watersheds in an effort to reduce fishing pressure on other species. Carp are omnivorous bottom feeders and tend to be repetitious. Once interested in a particular food, they will seek it out and ignore other offerings. Often these foods are surprising. For example, where a fruiting mulberry tree grows close to water's edge, carp often will congregate beneath its branches to gobble up dropping fruit.

WHERE AND WHEN: Carp are found in still and moving water virtually throughout the state. Spring and summer are the prime seasons for carp. Of note: while carp are characteristically vegetarians, they exhibit a marked preference for small worms and baby night crawlers when the water is still quite cold in early spring.

BAIT AND TACKLE: Carp can be caught from boat or shore with spinning or bait casting gear and bait typically consisting of kernel corn, prepared cornmeal balls or commercially available carp bait. The ideal rig is a seven foot medium weight spinning rod and reel with 8 lb. test line and a #6 baitholder hook, fished at bottom with sufficient weight to hold the bait immobile. A sliding egg sinker secured with a clamped split shot is recommended. The simplest bait is six to eight kernels of canned corn threaded on the hook, with additional kernels of corn broadcast into the water as chum. Significantly, keep the drag open while waiting for a bite, as the strike often will be violent and a closed drag will result either in a lost rod or a broken line in the blink of an eye.

STATE RECORD: The state record carp was caught by Billy Friedman in the South Branch of the Raritan River in 1995. It weighed a staggering 47 pounds. Parenthetically, records are kept for carp taken with bow and arrow but the authors have too much respect for carp to acknowledge this practice here.

FOOD VALUE: In certain cultures, carp are highly prized as table fare. They have fallen out of favor in most parts of the United States. ▪

Carp, Grass

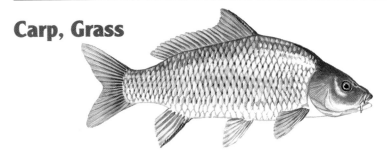

The grass carp, also called a white amur, is an invasive species stocked under controlled circumstances in New Jersey ponds and lakes to control undesirable aquatic vegetation. In order to prevent the unchecked spread of this species, a genetically altered form known as the "Triploid" was developed which is incapable of successful spawning. Since grass carp are able to consume as much as three times their own body weight in aquatic plants each day, they grow rapidly and can weigh upwards of 100 lbs. Aquatic plants are an essential part of the underwater environment as fish, waterfowl and furbearers utilize them for food and shelter. This explains the concern for unchecked breeding, since grass carp can virtually denude a body of water of aquatic vegetation.

IDENTIFICATION: The grass carp resembles the common carp in most respects. Their body color is dark olive shading to brownish-yellow on the sides, with a white belly (rather than yellowish) and large, slightly outlined scales. They resemble the common carp, as well, in their fighting abilities, which are considerable.

WHERE AND WHEN: Grass carp are sight feeders; thus fishing for them during the daylight hours is most productive. Since they are not naturally occurring and their reproduction is inhibited by the Triploid alteration, grass carp are usually found in stocked venues only. However, it is known that some escape into other bodies of water.

BAIT AND TACKLE: Fishing for grass carp is its own specialty. The fish are extremely wary, sensitive to motion on the bank and inevitably put off by sloppy casts and heavily weighted lines. Chumming is highly recommended, especially with canned corn or seed corn that has been allowed to ferment. Canned corn is a first rate bait, as are fruits (e.g., mulberries) that grow around the body of water. Stalking grass carp often involves seeing swirls in vegetation close to shore and quietly approaching the area for bait presentation.

STATE RECORD: The state record grass carp, a 55 pound 8 ounce beast, was caught in 2011 by angler Jack Demsey, Jr., fishing in Curlis Lake.

FOOD VALUE: The grass carp is edible but not highly prized as a food fish. ■

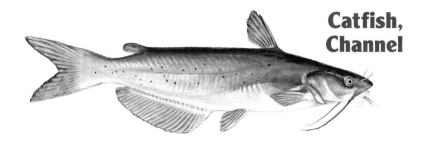

Catfish, Channel

The channel cat is the most widely sought of the catfish species commonly found in New Jersey and for good reason. They grow to significantly larger size than the other species, they fight harder and it is commonly thought, taste better.

IDENTIFICATION: The channel has a deeply forked tail with coloration ranging from olive brown to slate blue on the back, depending upon the color of the water they inhabit and gender, shading through gray to silvery white on the belly. Younger channels are irregularly marked with small black spots that disappear in larger adults.

WHERE AND WHEN: Channel cats generally prefer clear water streams, warm lakes and ponds but tolerate muddy water as well. They largely feed at night, ingesting a wide variety of small fish, snails, crawfish, aquatic plants and even algae.

The Hackettstown Hatchery annually raises some 45,000 channels that are stocked in well over 100 ponds and lakes throughout the state. The stocked fish range upwards in size from fry to well developed young adults measuring one to two feet in length. Naturally reproducing populations of channel cats also are known to exist in the Delaware River and its tidal tributaries, in the Raritan River and in Union Lake.

Significantly most stocked waters, including small ponds, are capable of producing trophy sized channels, as evidenced by the 26 lb.

leviathan caught in tiny Holmdel Park Pond in 1988.

BAIT AND TACKLE: While channels like the dark of night for feeding, they can be caught at any time of the day. The best approach is cut bait, canned corn, live shiners, stink bait or commercially prepared catfish bait fished at bottom, with chum distributed about the bait at intervals to attract fish and stimulate their appetites. Channels occasionally are caught on artificials, since they generally occupy the same waters and habitats as largemouth bass.

STATE RECORD: The state record for channel catfish is as longstanding as it is impressive. In 1978, Howard Hudson pulled a 33 pound 3 ounce lunker out of Lake Hopatcong.

FOOD VALUE: The channel is, as noted, the best table fare among the catfishes in New Jersey. It is no accident that this firm-fleshed catfish is one of the most widely farmed fish species in America. ■

Catfish, White

The white catfish is native to New Jersey and is sometimes called the forked tail cat because of its moderately forked tail.

DESCRIPTION: The white catfish is generally smaller than the channel catfish. Its sides are blue-gray and may be mottled. Its head is blunt and rounded and it lacks the dark spots commonly found on channels. The chin barbels are white or yellow.

WHERE AND WHEN: The white is found in the widest variety of venues, from large lakes and impoundments to the backwaters, pools and channels of rivers and streams. They also live in brackish bays and tidal sections of rivers and streams. The Delaware River and its tidal tributaries are prime white catfish waters, as are Spruce Run Reservoir, Union Lake, Boonton Reservoir and Budd Lake. Successful fishing for white catfish generally takes place from spring to early fall.

BAIT AND TACKLE: White catfish are bottom feeders, principally preying upon smaller fish. They also eat larval aquatic insects, crustaceans and some plant material. Fishing at bottom produces best results, preferably with a bottom rig consisting of relatively small hook with baitholder and a barrel sinker held 18 inches above the hook with a pinch-on split shot. Evening through dark of night are the most productive times to fish; night crawlers, chicken liver, cut fish and commercial stink baits are the best baits.

STATE RECORD: The state record white catfish, caught in Dallenbach Pond by Timothy Jasko in 2004, weighed 14 pounds 4 ounces.

FOOD VALUE: Smaller white catfish are excellent eating, especially when fried. ∎

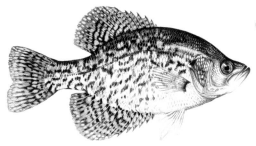

Crappie, Black

Black Crappies often are confused with their first cousins, the white crappie. However, the black is, as its name implies, considerably darker than the white, and more broadly distributed throughout the state. Many have commented on the crappie's feeding habits, none more eloquently than the Southern sage who observed: "Crappies are highly gregarious and feed ravenously when they feed at all. No fish in the world will outbite them when they take a notion."

DESCRIPTION: The black crappie, also commonly called calico bass, is deeper bodied than the white crappie and is silvery green in color, with irregular black blotches over most of its body.

WHERE AND WHEN: Crappies are well distributed in ponds, lakes and slow moving rivers throughout New Jersey. They prefer areas with little or no current and plentiful cover such as submerged timber or aquatic vegetation. Small fish feed on small aquatic invertebrates and change to a diet of fish, insects and larger invertebrates when they mature to adulthood. Some of the largest crappies we have seen have been caught in Spruce Run Reservoir, including a few dinner plate-sized specimens. Lake Musconetcong, Greenwood Lake, Lake Lenape, Assunpink Lake, Swartswood Lake and Lake Hopatcong also boast fine populations. Black crappies are quite active from early spring through late fall and again just after ice out, when they gravitate to shallow water to spawn.

Intrepid anglers who fish through the ice also take crappies in the dead of winter.

BAIT AND TACKLE: Anglers hunting crappies should look for structure. It has been said that the best place to fish is the precise spot where you are most likely to get your hook hung, and this is undeniably true. Crappies love structure and often schools of full bodied fish can be located in and around the branches of a recently submerged tree. A small shiner presented on a #6 wire hook beneath a slider float is our best prescription for taking crappies. Worms and killifish also will stimulate the crappie to strike, as will small, carefully presented jigs and flies.

STATE RECORD: A two pound black crappie is a bragging fish. However, the state record, caught in Pompton Lake in 1996 by Andy Tintle, weighed a whopping 4 pounds 8 ounces.

FOOD VALUE: The cotton white flesh of the Black crappie is hard to beat as table fare. ■

Crappie, White

Like its darker hued cousin, the white crappie is found in reservoirs, lakes, ponds and slow moving streams throughout New Jersey. The white also schools and at times feeds voraciously. However, there are significant differences between the two fish, aside from differences in appearance. First, unlike the black, the white crappie seems to prefer silted, turbid conditions over the clearer water and hard, clean bottoms habituated by blacks. On average, the white is the smaller of the two.

DESCRIPTION: Like other members of the sunfish family, white crappies are wide when viewed from the side but quite compressed when viewed head on. They are predominantly silvery green, with seven to nine dark vertical bars traversing the sides. All crappies have large mouths but the membrane behind the lips is thin and tears easily; thus the nickname "papermouth bass."

WHERE AND WHEN: White crappies can be caught virtually year round in slow moving streams and in lakes and ponds throughout the state. Generally cooler waters produce greater numbers of fish. March and November are considered the prime months to take crappies, with mild winter days also ideal. Crappies like cover such as submerged brush, stumps and tree roots.

BAIT AND TACKLE: An important key to catching white crappies is smallness: small live shiners, tiny jigs or tubes, small bobbers, small sinkers, light monofilament line. In addition, the lightest set is critical, since a hard jerk will tear the hook right through the crappie's thin mouth.

STATE RECORD: The state record white crappie weighed in at 3 pounds 11 ounces. It was caught in Mercer Lake by angler William Lewis in 2009.

FOOD VALUE: The white crappie is excellent table fare. As one noted crappie fisherman observed, "The crappie's palatability, wide distribution, adaptability and rapidity of growth combine to make him an eminently useful fish." ▓

Eel, American

The American Eel is a mysterious creature indeed. When sexually mature, eels in rivers, estuaries and tidal areas journey all the way to the Sargasso Sea, an area in the Atlantic Ocean south of Bermuda, to spawn and then to die. Eels remain in a larval state for about a year, drifting on ocean currents to coastal areas along their range. Eels support a valuable commercial food fishery, are widely used as bait for sport fish such as striped bass, and are an important food source for many fish and wildlife species.

DESCRIPTION: On reaching brackish water, the larvae begin to assume more recognizable shape. As they migrate upstream from estuaries to fresh water, they grow and change — from tiny glass eels to yellow eels to the mature phase, with the characteristic snake-like body, greenish silver coloration, extended dorsal fin and small pointed head.

WHERE AND WHEN: Eels are found statewide in streams, rivers, ponds and reservoirs, where they often spend winters buried in mud. They primarily prey upon smaller fishes, although they will eat anything they find. In lakes and reservoirs, eels are attracted to shallow coves with muddy bottoms. In moving water, they can be found in deeper pool areas with plenty of cover in the form of downed trees, brush piles and undercut banks.

BAIT AND TACKLE: Anglers seeking eels generally use small (e.g., #6 or #8) thin wire hooks on light line, with worms, small shiners or herring fished at or near bottom. Eels generally feed better at night, although they are taken during the day as well.

STATE RECORD: The state record American eel, weighing 6 pounds 13 ounces was caught by angler David J. Payne in 2005 while trout fishing in Round Valley Reservoir. He was casting live shiners from shore.

FOOD VALUE: Smoked eel has an excellent flavor and is favored by many. ▨

Fallfish

The fallfish is one of the most important species in New Jersey – not for its size or its fight or even its culinary appeal, but rather its place in the food chain. The largest of the minnows native to the state, it is one of the most populous fish in our waters and a critically important forage fish for game species like trout and bass.

DESCRIPTION: Fallfish, sometimes incorrectly called chub or creek chub, have dark backs and silver sides. Normally a few inches in length, they can reach nearly 17 inches.

WHERE AND WHEN: Fallfish are most abundant in clear small streams and rivers. They school with other fish species in shallow areas. They are most active from early spring to early summer during spawning, when males construct elaborate nests of gravel that can be up to six feet across. Adult fallfish feed on insects, other small fish and algae. They are usually caught accidentally, most often by anglers fishing for trout.

BAIT AND TACKLE: Fallfish eagerly take flies and bits of worm on small hooks, generally in clear streams.

STATE RECORD: There is no record for fallfish. However, while they average between three and 10 inches in length, it is known that these long lived minnows can reach several pounds in weight if left undisturbed.

FOOD VALUE: Fallfish appear more frequently in bait pails than on dinner tables. However, the occasional larger specimen is really quite tasty, especially when fried, if diners are willing to pick around its many y-bones. ▪

Muskellunge

The muskellunge is often referred to as "the fish of 10,000 casts" and not without reason. They are relatively rare, tough to find and even more difficult to catch. However, intensive and carefully managed stocking programs in New Jersey are establishing wonderful muskie fisheries that yield increasing numbers of trophy fish.

IDENTIFICATION: The muskellunge is the largest member of the pike family. It is a powerfully built elongated fish with jaws filled with razor sharp teeth. Its coloration is light green with irregular vertical bars and fins that range in coloration from brown to orange.

WHERE AND WHEN: The first muskellunge fishery in the state was developed in the Delaware River through the stocking efforts of the Pennsylvania Fish and Boat Commission in 1965. In 1993, the NJ Division of Fish and Wildlife began a successful rearing and stocking program that has yielded five additional fisheries: Greenwood Lake, Monksville Reservoir, Echo Lake Reservoir, Mountain Lake and Lake Hopatcong. Subsequently a partnership of Muskies Inc. and the Knee Deep Club has significantly increased the population of muskies in Lake Hopatcong. Muskellunge prefer habitat with clear, quiet water. Submerged weed beds interspersed with sunken stumps and logs comprise ideal muskie habitat. They are attack predators, lurking in their lairs awaiting prey, which ranges from fish, frogs and snakes to small birds and mammals.

BAIT AND TACKLE: Conventional wisdom does not always apply. It is thought that extremely large lures are needed to tempt muskies, but in fact many are caught on small plugs and spinners intended for walleye. It is said that you must troll fast to catch them, but in fact a speed of 4 to 6 miles an hour produces the most fish. It is often thought that artificials are virtually the only method for catching muskellunge when in fact, a large live sucker fished around the edge of a weedbed can be deadly. The secret to catching muskies is to have patience and be willing to try everything. Two concepts that are key: "sweeten" lures with fish scent, and use tackle and wire leaders heavy enough to land your trophy when it finally is hooked.

STATE RECORD: The state record muskellunge is a 42 pound 13 ounce beast caught through the ice at Monksville Reservoir in 1997 by Bob Neals.

FOOD VALUE: Muskellunge are seldom discussed as table fare. ■

Muskie, Tiger

Tiger muskies are a hybrid cross between the muskellunge and the northern pike and they exhibit characteristics of both parents.

DESCRIPTION: Tigers have elongated bodies with gray-green irregular narrow vertical dark markings on a light background, with stripes merging onto the back in an interlocking pattern. These markings distinguish them from the true strain muskellunge.

WHERE AND WHEN: Tiger muskies were experimentally raised and stocked by the state beginning in 1978, initially to learn (1) how pike and muskies would fare in New Jersey waters, and (2) what impact such large predatory fish would have on existing fish populations. The initial findings were encouraging, and over time tigers were stocked in 19 bodies of water in New Jersey, including Spruce Run, Budd Lake, Furnace Lake, Lake Hopatcong, Rancocas Creek, Little Swartswood Lake, Manasquan Reservoir and Greenwood Lake. In addition, Muskies Inc. teamed with the Knee Deep Club to stock tigers in Lake Hopatcong. In 2006 the program's emphasis was shifted entirely to true strain muskies. However, it is likely that significant numbers of 20 plus pound tigers still await anglers who are skilled and dedicated enough to pursue them.

BAIT AND TACKLE: Tiger muskies are daylight feeders and they become increasingly aggressive as waters warm in June, especially in and around the fringes of weed beds. They are less active as waters cool but still occasionally take live bait under the ice. Fishing for tigers is very similar to true strain muskellunge fishing in terms of lure selection (spinner baits, crank baits, jerk baits, etc.), although tigers seem to prefer somewhat smaller lures. In both instances, stout rods, good capacity reels and light wire leaders are indicated.

STATE RECORD: The state record tiger muskie, a 29 pound monster, was taken in 1990 in the Delaware River by angler Larry Migliarese.

FOOD VALUE: The tiger is not considered premium table fare. ■

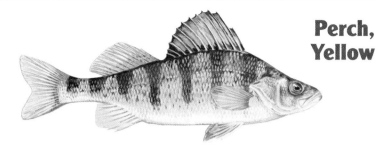

Perch, Yellow

The yellow perch is a hardy and extremely adaptable fish. While they prefer clear, fertile water, they can adjust to a wide variety of conditions, up to and including low oxygen levels that would suffocate bluegills, bass and walleye.

IDENTIFICATION: The yellow perch is perhaps the most easily identified panfish. The upper part of the head, back and sides are olive green to golden brown, shading to lighter yellow-green or yellow on the sides. The fins are pale yellow, becoming bright orange on males during breeding season. Dark scales form vertical stripes that narrow as they transit the body back to belly.

WHERE AND WHEN: The yellow perch fishery is well established in New Jersey, principally because of a huge historic boost from the New Jersey Division of Fish and Wildlife. In the 1920s, millions of fry were hatched and stocked in lakes, ponds and slow-moving rivers and streams throughout the state. Swartswood Lake, Malaga Lake, Greenwood Lake and Cranberry Lake are but several of the exceptionally reliable perch fishing venues today. Perch gravitate to underwater structure like stumps, fallen trees and the edges of weed beds. Minnows and small fish are the preferred prey of the mature yellow perch, which is itself an important prey species for larger predatory fish. Perch have a peculiar affinity for fish eyes. When an angler retrieves a suspended herring or shiner bereft of eyeballs, there is a very good chance yellow perch are around.

Perch feed throughout the year but become increasingly aggressive as the water temperature drops. The cool months of fall and early winter are excellent, and perhaps more perch than any other species are caught though the ice, quite often on a small jig tipped with a meal worm. The weeks just after ice out also produce great results.

BAIT AND TACKLE: Yellow perch generally are found within a foot or two of bottom. Therefore anglers concentrate on suspending bait (minnows, pieces of nightcrawlers, mealworms, wax worms, small cut bait) in this range. Small artificials typically used for crappie fishing are also effective when perch are feeding, most often worked with light one-handed spinning tackle.

STATE RECORD: The state record yellow perch, a fine 2 pound 6 ounce specimen, was caught in Holiday Lake in 1989 by angler Gene Engels.

FOOD VALUE: The yellow perch is absolutely delicious. Its white, flaky flesh may surpass even the walleye as a superb main course. ■

Pickerel, Chain

The chain pickerel is the only predatory warm water game fish native to New Jersey. It is an aggressive ambush predator competing for forage fish in many of the same venues as largemouth bass.

DESCRIPTION: The pickerel is distinguished from its relatives, the northern pike and muskellunge, by its prominent chain-like markings on a contrasting lighter green background. Its body is characteristically slender and its head is large, with a long, rounded snout full of sharp teeth.

WHERE AND WHEN: An extremely adaptable species, the pickerel thrives in a wide range of habitats from upland lakes and ponds to the acidic streams of the Jersey Pinelands and the coastal freshwater lakes near Cape May. Larger bodies with especially fine pickerel populations include Lake Lenape, Cranberry Lake, Lake Hopatcong and Swartswood Lake. The pickerel's main diet items are small fish, crayfish and frogs. Their ambush style of feeding requires cover. Consequently they most often are found in weedy patches in streams, ponds, lakes and rivers where they can lurk until prey swim by.

BAIT AND TACKLE: Pickerel are truly game fish for all seasons. Anglers score well from early Spring right through winter with live baits and a wide variety of spinnerbaits, topwater lures, jerkbaits and plastics worked around lily pads, downed trees and manmade structures.

In winter "chains" are among the most active feeders through the ice, taking a wide variety of natural and artificial lures. Light spinning tackle is recommended when casting or trolling. Tip ups are commonly used when fishing live bait through the ice.

STATE RECORD: The state record for chain pickerel is one of long standing, predated only by the record landlocked salmon. In 1957, angler Frank McGovern landed a 9 pound 3 ounce beauty in Lower Aetna Lake.

FOOD VALUE: The chain pickerel is not as welcomed at the dining table as some other game fish due to its profusion of small y bones. However, for those not put off by bones, the meat is sweet, white and flaky.

Pickerel, Redfin

The redfin pickerel is the smallest member of the pike family and is relatively uncommon in New Jersey. When caught, it often is mistakenly identified as a chain pickerel, although the differences are marked.

DESCRIPTION: The redfin is generally smaller and chunkier than the chain, with distinctive orange to red fin coloration that gives it its name. In addition, the light areas between dark bands are generally narrower on the redfin than on the chain.

WHERE AND WHEN: Like chains, redfin pickerel are ambush predators that usually can be found in shallow bays of lakes or sluggish streams with plenty of vegetation. They are found occasionally in Lake Lenape, Lake Assunpink, Cranberry Lake, Lake Hopatcong, Carnegie Lake and the Musconetcong River, although less frequently in all cases than the chain pickerel.

BAIT AND TACKLE: Anglers don't usually target redfins because of their relative scarcity and their small size. When caught, they generally have responded to shiners, killies, spinners or small plastic baits fished close to weed beds or lily pads, cast in search of bass or crappies.

STATE RECORD: The state record redfin pickerel, weighing a surprising 1 pound 13 ounces, was caught in Lake Assunpink in 1982 by angler Gerald Humphrey.

FOOD VALUE: Because of their small size, bony structure and scarcity, redfins are not generally thought of as a food fish. ■

Pike, Northern

The northern pike is a voracious predator and a much-pursued game fish, not least because of the large size they attain in Jersey waters. They are thought to be the most widely distributed freshwater game fish in the world.

IDENTIFICATION: Northerns have a pointed snout in a long, flattened head, an elongated body and a mouth full of extremely sharp teeth slanted inward for holding and tearing prey. Their colors range from shades of green to brown, with gold flecks and white bellies. Adult northerns feed on other fish, crayfish and frogs and have even been observed attacking muskrats and birds.

WHERE AND WHEN: Northerns like relatively shallow weedy areas of lakes and slow moving rivers, although they are adaptable to a variety of waters. They are regularly stocked in lakes (Pompton, Budd, Cranberry, Spruce Run, Farrington and Deal) and rivers, to include the Millstone, Pompton and Passaic. Cool weather yields the best pike fishing. The pre-spawn period just after ice-out and after spawning late in March are the most productive periods, usually in very shallow water.

BAIT AND TACKLE: Crankbaits, spoons and spinnerbaits, cast but most especially trolled, induce northern pike to strike. However, nothing is as reliable as large shiners fished at or near bottom in pockets of weedy areas in lakes and around structure and in deeper holes in rivers. Pike often are hooked on the outsides of their mouths since they typically grab the bait sideways and attempt to swim away. When bait is swallowed, a bitten-through monofilament leader is a familiar result.

STATE RECORD: The state record northern pike is a 30 pound 8.5 ounce monster caught in Pompton Lake by John Viglione in 2009.

FOOD VALUE: While not esteemed as table fare because of a profusion of bones, the northern is in fact quite tasty when filleted and prepared properly. ▧

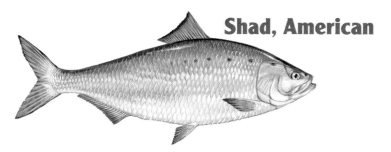

Shad, American

The American Shad was an important fish species in New Jersey long before the first settlers arrived, and today, with the Delaware River benefitting so dramatically from the Clean Water Act, hundreds of thousands of feisty adult shad are making their way upstream each spring to spawn. Significantly, improving water quality is helping to create shad fisheries in other New Jersey waters as well, prominently to include the Raritan River and Rancocas Creek.

IDENTIFICATION: The American shad is actually the largest member of the herring family. It has a blue gray back and silver body, and unlike other herring, a mouth that extends to the back of the eye. Like other herring, the shad is primarily a plankton feeder, but will eat small shrimp, fish eggs and occasionally small fish.

WHERE AND WHEN: After spawning, the juveniles remain in the river until fall. They then migrate downstream to the ocean when they are approximately two to three inches in length. In three to six years, they return to freshwater to spawn, generally weighing four to eight pounds. Earliest spawning begins somewhere south of the Delaware Water Gap but many fish press on to the New York State line and beyond before completing the spawning process. Unlike salmon, some shad retain the ability to survive the spawning run and return to the sea. It is thought that as many as 10% of spawning shad in New Jersey propagate two or more times.

BAIT AND TACKLE: As the shad run ascends to the mid reaches of the Delaware, each spring fishing boats can be seen anchored almost bank to bank as anglers ply the waters with shad darts or flutter spoons, sometimes fished on downriggers to keep the lure at the desired depth and location. Shad also are caught by anglers casting from shore in favorite spots from Lambertville up to the Water Gap.

STATE RECORD: Not surprisingly, the state record shad, an 11 pound 1 ounce bruiser was caught in the Delaware River. The lucky angler was Charles Mower, who set the record in 1984.

FOOD VALUE: The shad can be boiled, baked and if filleted, fried with equal gustatory pleasure. The roe is considered a delicacy. ▧

Striped Bass, Hybrid

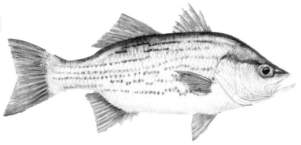

The hybrid striped bass is a rare example of man improving upon nature. A cross between a white bass and a true striped bass, the hybrid combines the best characteristics of both fish. It attacks baitfish with unmatched ferocity and fights like nothing else in fresh water, from the first second of its surging strike to the moment it is lifted exhausted into the boat. In addition, the hybrid grows very fast, from fingerling size to 16 inches by its second year, and potentially up to 20 lbs. in seven years.

The hybrid was first produced in the deep South in the mid 1960s when biologists from Tennessee and South Carolina fertilized eggs from striped bass with sperm from white bass. The resulting hybrid was first stocked in Cherokee Lake in Tennessee; consequently the hybrid is sometimes called a Cherokee bass. In New Jersey, hybrids were first stocked in Lake Hopatcong in the early 1980s by the always innovative Knee Deep Club, and in Assunpink Lake, Cranberry Lake and Union Lake by the N. J. Division of Fish and Wildlife in 1984.

DESCRIPTION: The hybrid bass is characterized by lateral stripes similar to those of the true strain striper. However, the hybrid's stripes are generally broken behind the pectoral fin and below the lateral line. Their color graduates from silver and black to white underneath.

WHERE AND WHEN: Hybrid bass thrive in deep lakes with plenty of open water; consequently the state annually stocks thousands of four inch fingerlings in Spruce Run Reser-

voir, Lake Hopatcong, and the Manasquan Reservoir. As the popularity of the hybrid increases, additional fish are stocked in a variety of venues by private clubs. Hybrids provide a thrill that is unique in freshwater fishing in New Jersey when a feeding frenzy of big fish crash into surfacing alewife herring. Gulls dive into the resulting melee and when the gulls are heading toward the angler's baited lines, he has but seconds to prepare for screaming drag, long tearing runs and wildly pulsating rods. The most productive season for hybrid fishing ranges from late spring to early fall.

BAIT AND TACKLE: A stout one hand spinning outfit is recommended, fished with the drag always fully open in anticipation of the strike. The preferred live bait is the alewife herring, although hybrids will also take shiners, chicken livers and the occasional nightcrawler. The most successful hybrid anglers troll, drift fish or double anchor. Live baits are usually live lined or suspended just above the thermocline. An effective method is the use of slider floats fished away from the boat at carefully calibrated depths.

STATE RECORD: The state record hybrid, a 16 pound 4 ounce beast, was taken in Culver Lake by angler Bill Schmidt in 1999.

FOOD VALUE: The hybrid is prized as table fare, its dense, snow-white filets excellent whether baked, broiled, grilled or fried. However, some anglers consider taking hybrid bass for the table something akin to a sportsman's sin. ▪

Sunfish, Pumpkinseed

The pumpkinseed sunfish, also called the common sunfish, is said to be shaped like a pumpkin seed and colored like a pumpkin; hence its name.

IDENTIFICATION: The pumpkinseed is a colorful slab-sided fish with an orange to yellow belly, many small orange to brown spots scattered over its side and an identifying red-orange spot on its ear flap.

WHERE AND WHEN: Pumpkinseeds are widely distributed throughout the state, generally preferring clear, non-flowing water and substrates of organic debris and dense submerged aquatic vegetation. Like the bluegill, the common sunfish is a schooling fish which takes bait easily because of its competitive nature. They tend to stay near shore and are most active during the day, resting near bottom in protected areas at night. They feed on insects, mosquito larva, small crustaceans and minnow fry.

Pumpkinseeds are among the most accommodating of fish, especially for the young angler. Because they tend to remain in the shallows and feed all day, they are relatively easy to catch from shore. They are generally quite abundant, they are taken on the simplest and most readily available baits (garden worms, bits of bread, insects) and they fight aggressively when hooked. And they are caught in all weathers, most especially sunny bluebird days when other fish are disinterested but also through the ice in the dead of winter.

BAIT AND TACKLE: Fishing for the common sunfish is an exercise in simplicity. A small hook, a length of monofilament line, a bobber and pinch-on sinker plus a piece of worm and the angler is in business. Because these fish congregate near shore, the time honored cane pole is often as utilitarian as a fine casting outfit.

STATE RECORD: The state record pumpkinseed, weighing 1 pound 8 ounce, was caught in a private farm pond in 1987 by Daryl Donalson.

FOOD VALUE: Typically 5 to 8 inches long, the pumpkinseed requires a good deal of effort to prepare for the table but is nonetheless worth the effort.

Sunfish, Redbreast

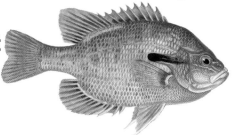

As its name implies, the redbreast sunfish is recognized by its flaming bright colored breast and sides.

IDENTIFICATION: The redbreast's second name, long ear sunfish, comes from its elongated gill flap terminating in a long black spot. This characteristic, together with bright orange coloration, are spot-on identifiers.

WHERE AND WHEN: Redbreasts gravitate to the same habitats as smallmouth bass; that is, clear flowing rivers like the Delaware and streams with hard substrate bottoms. However, like bluegills, they also are found in the widest variety of venues, from small creeks to massive reservoirs. They feed on aquatic insects and terrestrial insects that fall into the water, plus very small fish and crayfish. Redbreasts are generally not caught in numbers like the aggressive schooling bluegills or pumpkinseeds. The primary reason is that in the summer, when fishing in ponds and lakes is most popular, the redbreast sunfish tend to be loners, only schooling up when the water cools.

BAIT AND TACKLE: Fishing for redbreasts is a small-hook-and-bobber affair, no different from the other sunfish. Worms are the traditional bait for these scrappy sunfish, but at times they show a preference for small live shiners.

STATE RECORD: There is no state record registered for redbreast sunnies.

FOOD VALUE: In New Jersey, redbreasts are generally thought to be too small to be useful as food. However, in the deep South where they grow to significant proportions, they are considered a delicacy. ▉

Walleye

The walleye is a target fish for an ever-growing number of New Jersey anglers in a relatively limited number of venues. Healthy populations thrive in the Delaware River and in Lake Hopatcong, Monksville Reservoir, Greenwood Lake and Swartswood Lake, all producing sizeable fish in the five to nine pound range.

IDENTIFICATION: The walleye is most easily identified by its outsized pearlescent eyes which help them to see and feed in murky water and at night. Their coloration ranges from golden yellow to dark olive drab, broken up by five darker saddles that extend upward from white belly to the upper sides.

WHERE AND WHEN: The walleye program began in 1989 when the Hacketstown Hatchery received more than 3 million eggs from sources in Pennsylvania, New York and Canada. Over one million fry were originally stocked in Monksville Reservoir. Subsequently Lake Hopatcong, Greenwood Lake and Swartswood Lake were added to the program. Cannistear Lake is the latest recipient of walleye fry and fingerlings. In a recent stocking year, almost 2 million fry and fingerlings were stocked.

Fishing for walleye always begins with a consciousness of light. Because their large eyes are sensitive to light, the best times to fish are very early morning, evening and from dusk to midnight. Cloudy days are inevitably better than bluebird days, and deeper, darker water better than shallow water during the day.

BAIT AND TACKLE: Walleye can be taken on small crankbaits, small jigs and plastic worms around gravel ledges, points and submerged humps. Walleyes also are partial to small nightcrawlers, alewife herring and shiners, fished most productively near bottom or on slider floats (slip bobbers) to keep bait at the right depth.

STATE RECORD: The state record walleye, caught in the Delaware River by George Fundell in 1993, tipped the scales at 13 pounds 9 ounces.

FOOD VALUE: As a food fish the walleye may have no equal in fresh water. The white flaky flesh is absolutely delicious. ▪

New Jersey's Marine Fishery

I n deep blue-water canyons off the coast of New Jersey, enormous tuna, marlin and sharks ply the edge of the continental shelf in search of prey. Seventy miles closer to shore, schools of ravenous bluefish relentlessly pursue bunker and other forage fish in places like Five Fathom Bank, Barnegat Inlet, Shrewsbury Rocks and Raritan Bay. Big striped bass provide exciting action for surf casters all along the state's 210 miles of beaches. And in between the beaches and canyons, super abundant stocks of sea bass, blackfish, porgy, ling, croaker and fluke provide even more spectacular recreational marine fishing opportunities for 500,000 salt water anglers each year. Fishing from charter boats and party boats, piers and docks, beaches and rocky shorelines, New Jersey anglers annually land more than 14 million pounds of fish, ranking New Jersey third in recreational fish landings among the 14 Atlantic coastal states.

The state's fortuitous geography places anglers in a zone where both north coast and south coast species spend good chunks of time in Jersey's near and offshore waters. The angling choices include 40 species of inshore, offshore and pelagic fish that are most popularly sought, and caught, among 336 species of finfish in our waters. Indeed, the variety is such that the greatest challenge anglers face may very well be deciding which fish to target and where to fish for them.

The information provided in this book will surely help anglers meet that challenge, as will the authors' other book, *Gone Fishin': The 100 Best Spots in New Jersey.* Readers also are encouraged to explore the NJDEP and Division of Fish and Wildlife websites. The Division of Fish and Wildlife's www.njfishandwildlife.com has many valuable marine fishing information gems including *A Guide to Fishing and Diving New Jersey's Reefs, NJ Boat Ramp Guide, Party and Charter Boat Directory* and the *Guide to NJ's Saltwater Fishing.* A new free app provides this information on Smartphones while on the water.

Whether you're looking for a relaxing day of chunking for stripers or blues off the beach, drifting the bay for fluke, reef fishing for tog or sea bass or plying the Canyons for marlin or tuna, New Jersey will surely not disappoint when it comes to the quantity and quality of saltwater fishing action.

Jim Sciascia
Chief of Information and Education
New Jersey Division of Fish & Wildlife

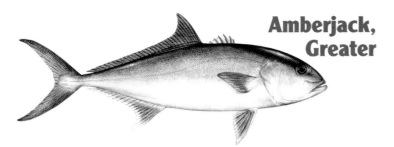

Amberjack, Greater

The Greater Amberjack is an extremely powerful member of the jack family and relatively rare in New Jersey waters. More than 200,000 anglers signed up for the saltwater registry in the state for 2012 and chances are that less than one hundred of them will have caught an "AJ" by year's end. And since they are so incredibly strong, the angler who has managed to hook one may well be broken off without ever knowing what fish swam away with his hook.

DESCRIPTION: AJ's are long and powerful with a wide circumference. A yellowish bar that runs from eye to tail distinguishes this fish from other jacks. The AJ also has an identifying black stripe from the mouth back through the eye to the dorsal fin.

WHERE AND WHEN: The best time and place to find Amberjacks is summer on deepwater wrecks in Southern New Jersey waters. Some are occasionally found at other times and places, but summer and south are the most reliable guides.

BAIT AND TACKLE: Live bait and heavy stand-up rods and reels are indispensable for these powerful and seemingly inexhaustible fish. They run hard and long and often wear anglers down before they even begin to tire. Once over a wreck, drop a live bait to bottom, reel up 10 to 20 feet and wait. If an "AJ" is near, he will make his presence known quickly.

STATE RECORD: The heaviest New Jersey amberjack weighed 85 pounds even and was taken off Cape May by Edwin Metzer in 1993.

FOOD VALUE: Many amberjacks today have parasites, a fact that is simple to determine when they are filleted at the dock. The AJ's that are free of parasites make good eating, especially when broiled. ▧

Bass, Black Sea

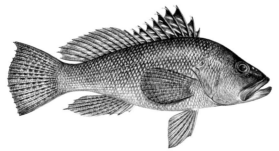

Not generally known is the fact that the black sea bass is actually a member of the grouper family. It is widely sought because it is plentiful and makes fine dining. Seasonal closings plus carefully regulated size and bag limits allow sea bass to multiply and prosper.

DESCRIPTION: Although they are called "black" sea bass, most are actually more brownish or dark gray than black. Often called "knuckleheads," they form bluish knots on the tops of their heads while in spawning phase. Of note: most sea bass begin life as females and then change to males within two to five years to accommodate reproduction requirements.

WHERE AND WHEN: Undersized sea bass are caught inshore each summer in saltwater rivers and bays. It should be noted that most sea bass contain a few slim filaments that protrude out beyond the normal length of the tail. Sea bass are measured to the longest part of the tail *excluding* these filaments. Offshore wrecks, artificial reefs and other rough bottom structure are favored by sea bass. When reeled up too quickly from deep water, a sea bass may suffer the bends, as evidenced by its air bladder protruding from its mouth. If the fish is to be released, a small needle-like venting device is used to pierce the air bladder so the fish can be safely returned to the water.

BAIT AND TACKLE: Some of the larger sea bass are caught with small crabs as bait. However, the great majority are taken with a

squid strip or piece of clam. Offset hooks in sizes 2/0 or 3/0 are preferred. (Smaller hooks may produce a higher number of very small fish, which benefits neither angler nor fish.) Since much of the action occurs in deep water, a conventional boat rod and reel with 30-lb. test line is recommended. In shallower water, a baitcasting outfit with 20 lb. test line will suffice.

STATE RECORD: In 2010, Andrew A. Merindino boated an 8 pound 4.5 ounce beauty off Cape May. No venting device was required to puncture its air bladder, since this fine fish went home with Andrew after being certified as a state record.

FOOD VALUE: Among the most widely sought species along the New Jersey coast, the black sea bass is certain to satisfy a gourmet's palate. Sea bass are a featured delicacy, cooked whole, in Chinese restaurants. ■

Bluefish

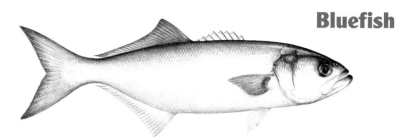

Bluefish are spectacular fighting machines much loved by New Jersey anglers, even when they take the last live eel or bunker head intended for a big striped bass.

DESCRIPTION: Bluefish are long and lean in the spring when they head north from southern waters. Called "racers" because of their slim profiles, they quickly grow in circumference as they fatten up in our rivers and bays. Bluefish have large mouths with prominent teeth and a forked tail. They are blue or black on top, shading to silvery white on their bellies.

WHERE AND WHEN: Other than for a week or two each summer when spawning, blues are available both inshore and offshore, wherever they find abundant forage fish.

BAIT AND TACKLE: Tackle choices vary with circumstances. On a private boat, relatively light tackle may be preferred. On a head boat, standard party boat tackle is the rule to prevent unnecessary tangles. Many bluefish are caught from drifting boats with ground bunker chum used to attract fish to chunk-baited wired hooks. Wire leaders are essential since blues chop through monofilament with ease. Blues also are caught while jigging and trolling.

STATE RECORD: The heaviest bluefish recorded in New Jersey was a 27 pound 1 ounce fish caught at the Five Fathom Bank in 1997 by angler Roger Kastorsky.

FOOD VALUE: Eating bluefish is an acquired taste, since the flesh is somewhat strong tasting. However, when quickly cleaned and especially when fried, bluefish can be more than acceptable table fare. Of note: bluefish do not take well to freezing so they should be cooked shortly after being caught. ■

Bonito, Atlantic

This fish is, in fact, an "Atlantic Bonito." Down south, some call a false albacore/little tunny" a bonito but they are referring to a completely different fish.

DESCRIPTION: Our bonito is built like a tuna but generally smaller in size. Normally weighing less than ten pounds, they make up for their small stature with superb fighting ability. They are silvery blue with a white belly and horizontal stripes along their entire back.

WHERE AND WHEN: Often found in schools and frequently mixed in with bluefish and false albacore, bonito can be found in open ocean as well as around reefs and wrecks. Summer is the most productive time to fish for bonito.

BAIT AND TACKLE: Lures produce strikes, but most bonito are taken on bait. One or two spearing hooked through the eye sockets may be most productive. Because these fish are much more "line shy" than bluefish or false albacore, a smallish hook — size 1/0 to 2/0 — is recommended. Boat tackle is standard on head boats but on private craft, lighter spinning gear can provide superb action.

STATE RECORD: The record for bonito is long-standing. In 1945, Frank Lykes, Jr. set the record when he boated a 13 lb. 8 oz. beauty off Sandy Hook.

FOOD VALUE: The meat of the bonito is far whiter than most fish taken in the same water. Baked or broiled, a fresh fillet of bonito is quite delicious. ■

Cobia

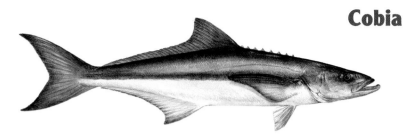

Cobia are generally found in warm-temperate waters; however, they are able to tolerate a wide range of temperatures and make seasonal migrations northward along the coasts in search of comfortable water. These migrations bring them as far north as New Jersey.

DESCRIPTION: Cobia are long, slim fish with dark lateral stripes extending through the eye to the tail. Their bodies are brown grading to white on the belly and smooth with small scales. Most fins on mature fish are a dark brown.

WHERE AND WHEN: Cobia caught in New Jersey are usually found in the state's southernmost waters, at the northern extreme of their migration patterns. Cobia are intensely curious fish and exhibit no fear of boats. They frequently are found around wrecks, pilings and buoys. They also follow and swim below larger species such as sharks, turtles and rays in the interest of scavenging a meal.

BAIT AND TACKLE: Medium heavy tackle is recommended for cobia, which can weigh 30 pounds or more. Cobia feed primarily on smaller fish as well as crabs and squid. Sight casting with live bait accounts for most hookups, although jigs and large streamer flies also produce results. The curiosity of these fish can often be used against them as they swim around the boat examining other fighting fish.

STATE RECORD: The state record "cobe," an 87 pound bruiser, was caught off Sea Bright by John Sanchuk in 1999. This was an exception proving a rule, since most Jersey cobia are, as noted, taken well to the south.

FOOD VALUE: Excellent, fresh or smoked, grilled or poached. The fillets are quite dense and take a bit longer to cook through than most fish. For optimum taste, the dark layer of flesh under the skin should be carefully removed when cleaning. ■

Codfish

Years ago, New Jersey's coastal waters teemed with codfish as fall turned to winter. However, stocks of cod diminished sharply as foreign factory ships depleted our waters of whiting, an important forage fish, and no doubt of codfish as well. Newly enacted laws finally closed our waters to the factory ships, and codfish stocks have rebounded sharply.

DESCRIPTION: Codfish are easy to identify. The fish caught in New Jersey are green with white bellies and have three separate soft-rayed dorsal fins and two separate soft-rayed anal fins. Codfish are long lived and can achieve surprising size, growing to five feet or more in length. However, the average fish in our waters is more likely to weigh between five and 10 pounds.

WHERE AND WHEN: Cod are bottom oriented and prefer cold, deep water. They are caught in depths generally ranging from 60 feet down to 300 feet, with 100 or more feet being the "gold standard." They prefer hard struct- ure, so ship wrecks, artificial reefs and natural deepwater reefs are prime target areas. Late fall to early spring define the prime times to take codfish, although cod are occasionally taken in deep holes year round.

BAIT AND TACKLE: While cod are not classic fighting fish, a 20 pounder still will bend your rod and give you a tussle. Consequently, conventional rods and reels with 30 pound test line or heavier are indicated. Some anglers use two hook bait rigs, with one hook tied in well above an 8 to 12 ounce bank sinker and a second just above the sinker knot. Each hook, size 5/0 to 7/0, is attached via a dropper loop. Others prefer heavy jigs, often with a red or green teaser hook tied two feet above the jig. Skimmer clam is the number one bait, although a fillet of mackerel or herring also can produce results.

STATE RECORD: Other than pelagics like tuna and some sharks, few New Jersey state records approach the size of a cod. Caught in 1967 by Joseph Chesla out of Brielle, the top cod weighed 81 pounds.

FOOD VALUE: Codfish are excellent eating. The lightly flavored flesh can be broiled, baked, fried or poached, or cooked in chowders or fish cakes. Charter captains recommend that cod be bled, gutted and iced as soon as they are caught to preserve their delicate flavor. ■

Croaker, Atlantic

The American croaker is closely related to red and black drum, weakfish, spotted sea trout and spot. Croakers are popular with anglers because of their abundant numbers, accessibility and hardy nature. They get their name from the croaking sound they make by vibrating their air bladders with special muscles.

DESCRIPTION: Croakers are generally less than two pounds in size, with somewhat compressed silvery bodies and underslung mouths to facilitate bottom feeding. The upper dorsal side has variable brassy spots that form wavy bars in younger fish, but become less pronounced in larger adults.

WHERE AND WHEN: Croakers are among the first fish to be caught in South Jersey waters each spring and appear in numbers further north to Raritan Bay as the water warms in summer. They are especially abundant in Delaware Bay. They are found on mud, sand and shell bottoms of coastal estuaries where they feed on worms, grass shrimp and occasionally small fishes. They are regularly caught from jetties, piers, anchored boats in bays and inlets and from the surf.

BAIT AND TACKLE: Bait casting and spinning gear are well suited to croaker fishing. Two hook rigs work well, with one hook riding above and the other below the sinker. Hooks should be small — ideally a size 4 offset hook with bait holders so that the small bait offering will stay on the hook. A small piece of clam, worm or shedder crab will produce good results. Surf casters generally use pyramid shaped sinkers with sufficient weight to maintain contact with bottom.

STATE RECORD: The state record croaker was caught in Delaware Bay in 1981 by angler Frederick Brown. It weighed a surprising 5 pounds 8 ounces.

FOOD VALUE: Croakers make a tasty meal. The smaller ones generally are cooked whole, but fish that reach a pound or more can be filleted. Of note: even when skillfully filleted, it is virtually impossible to remove all of the small bones, so diners should exercise a bit of caution. ■

Cunner

The cunner, also called sea perch, closely resembles its more highly prized relative, the blackfish, and like the blackfish, it has a second and if anything, a more popularly used name. The cunner is most often referred to as the "bergall," just as the black is often called a "tautog," or simply "tog." Cunner often swim with the larger togs, picking off bits of crab and shellfish the blackfish accidentally drop.

DESCRIPTION: The cunner has a slimmer body, more pointed snout and thinner lips than the tautog. They vary in coloration from greenish to reddish/brown, depending upon habitat, and they have scales on their gill plates, another characteristic that distinguishes them from their larger cousins.

WHERE AND WHEN: Cunners are reef system inhabitants, regularly relating to reefs and rocks. They feed actively during daylight hours but seek the shelter of reefs, rock outcroppings or stands of kelp for protection at night, when they become largely quiescent. In winter they become less active and many migrate to seasonal habitats in deeper water until coastal waters warm again. As to specific location at any given time, it is likely that if the angler locates blackfish, cunner will be nearby.

BAIT AND TACKLE: Cunners are normally a by catch rather than a targeted species. However, they fight well for their size and can be fun to catch, especially for younger anglers. A light spinning rod, a hook as small as a size 6 and a small strip of clam for bait will produce good results. Caution: when removing a hook, use care to avoid the bergall's sharp teeth and gill plates.

STATE RECORD: In 2006, well known writer/ angler Nick Honachefsky of Mantoloking caught the state and world record cunner, beating the previous record by nearly a pound. His fish was 16 inches long and weighed 2 pounds 9 ounces. That record seemed destined to stand for a very long time, but it was beaten in 2012 when Raul de la Prida caught a 3 pound ½ ounce cunner fishing on the Norma K III out of Point Pleasant.

FOOD VALUE: Larger cunner can be filleted and will produce a tasty meal. Smaller ones can be pan or oven fried or baked whole with similar results. ■

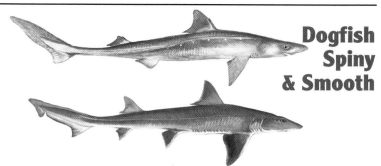

Dogfish
Spiny
& Smooth

Dogfish is a generic name for a large number of small, generally harmless and unaggressive sharks. The two most common dogfish in Jersey waters are the spiny and the smooth. They are called dogfish because they travel and hunt in packs, at times segregated by sex and age. They are seldom targeted by anglers and are most often caught inadvertently by boats seeking cod, ling and bluefish. Dogfish are thought to be the world's most abundant shark.

DESCRIPTION: The spiny dogfish, a protected species in our waters, is grey in color and has a sharp spike/spine that is found in front of each of its two dorsal fins. The spine is sharp and slightly toxic, not unlike the sharp spines of a catfish. Another identifying characteristic is a row of small white dots that run along its sides. The smooth dogfish is darker in color and lacks the spines of its "spiny" cousin. Also, while the skin of a spiny dogfish is rough to the touch, the skin of a smooth is a continuous even surface; hence its name.

WHERE AND WHEN: Dogfish can be found anywhere in the water column offshore, but they seldom enter the upper reaches of estuaries and never occur in fresh water. As noted, they often are caught offshore when baitfishing for more desirable species; in fact, a dozen may be caught before the angler gets his bait taken by a cod or ling. In summer they cruise closer to shore, often taking baits intended for fluke, and in the fall, they bedevil boats after big "slammer" blues, taking bait after bait before the blues can get to them.

BAIT AND TACKLE: As noted dogfish are most often taken by anglers interested in other fish. However, they can grow to considerable size, so party boat rods and reels are needed to land them. As to bait, dogfish are not particular. Cut bait, clams, crabs and virtually any other bait that happens to be at hand will entice dogfish.

STATE RECORD: The record spiny dogfish weighed 15 pounds 12 ounces. It was caught by Jeff Pennick off Cape May in 1990. The record smooth dogfish weighed 19 pounds 9 ounces and was caught by Richard A. Proot off Mantoloking in 2010.

FOOD VALUE: In North America dogfish are generally not considered good to eat although if killed and cleaned immediately after being boated, the flesh isn't at all bad. If not immediately bled, the flesh tends to sour quickly. Of note: in Europe, dogfish often are served as "fish and chips" and some years ago, one party boat's mate was said to have sold them to a well known "fish and chips" chain in New York for the same purpose. ■

Dolphin / Mahi Mahi

Dolphin are among the fastest growing fish in the ocean, achieving sexual maturity and considerable size quickly. Not to be confused with porpoises – the ocean-going mammal also called dolphin – the beautifully iridescent dolphin fish are called mahi mahi, the Hawaiian word for very strong, and sometimes, dorado.

DESCRIPTION: Brilliantly colored, mahi mahi light up in a rainbow of vivid yellows, greens and blues when they strike. Adult males are distinguished from females by prominent foreheads. They feed on crabs, squid, mackerel and other forage fish and are most commonly found in surface water.

WHERE AND WHEN: Sport fishermen occasionally take mahi mahi in summer while trolling as close in to the beach as ten miles. However, it is likely that as many as 90% of all mahi mahi caught in New Jersey waters are taken out around the various canyons where tuna hunters prowl. Of note: anglers look for lobster pot buoy markers offshore, since schools of mahi mahi are known to lurk nearby.

BAIT AND TACKLE: Small lures cast to schooling fish, especially when worked near debris such as floating wood and around buoys, can be quite productive. Spinning gear is perfectly adequate to catch these beautiful, exciting fish. Of note: when hooked, a dolphin often will attract curious "schoolmates." Therefore anglers often avoid bringing them to the boat before companions can cast to trailing fish.

STATE RECORD: The largest mahi mahi caught in New Jersey's waters weighed 63 pounds 3 ounces. It was landed by Scott Smith Jr. at the Baltimore Canyon in 1974.

FOOD VALUE: Mahi mahi is a familiar menu item in many fine restaurants and is preferred by many people to any other fish. The flesh is quite delicate, soft and tasty. As with many fish that swim higher in the water column, they have a dark layer of bloody flesh right under the skin that should be cut away before cooking. ■

Drum, Black

The black drum is the largest inshore fish in New Jersey waters, with 60 or 70 pound fish not unusual. Like other members of the croaker family, blacks produce croaking or drumming sounds, an ability more highly developed in the black drum than in the red drum or Atlantic croaker. In fact, the drumming is sufficiently loud that anglers can sometimes hear sounds from fish below their boats.

DESCRIPTION: The black drum is a chunky, high-backed fish with many barbels on the lower jaws. Their coloration varies greatly with conditions. Those living in muddy waters typically have dark gray or bronze-colored backs and sides, while coloration lightens in clearer, cleaner habitats. Although drum in excess of 30 pounds are generally referred to as "bull" drum, size is not a reliable predictor of gender, since large specimens can be either male or female. Black drum in the one to five pound class are often taken inshore.

WHERE AND WHEN: Black drum have been reported as far north as Raritan Bay but Delaware Bay is where they appear most consistently and in largest numbers. Occasionally a black drum will be caught surfcasting, but most are caught from charter and party boats. The most productive time of year is May and June.

BAIT AND TACKLE: Heavy gear is required, not only because of the huge size of "bull" blacks, but also because they often feed on a strong moving tide. The preferred baits are whole fresh clams or shedder crabs on a single 8/0 to 12/0 hook and a 50 lb. leader, with a sufficiently heavy sinker to hold bottom.

STATE RECORD: The black drum is a member of that very exclusive list, along with sharks and tuna, of fish in our waters that can exceed 100 pounds. The state record, weighing 109 pounds, was caught in Delaware Bay in 2008 by angler Nick Henry.

FOOD VALUE: Large black drum are not desirable for the table and should be carefully released. However, drum weighing less than five pounds, cleaned and prepared properly, are thought by some to be better than such "choice" fish as flounder. The recommended cooking method is rolling filets in cornmeal and frying. ■

Drum, Red

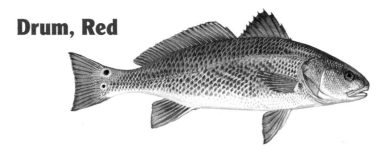

Red drum are related to black drum, spotted seatrout, weakfish and croakers, most of which also make drumming sounds. The red's distinctive black spots near its tail are believed to confuse predators into attacking its tail rather than its head, allowing it to escape. Red drum are caught in New Jersey much less frequently than their immediate relatives, the black drum.

DESCRIPTION: Red drum, also known as redfish or simply "reds," are reddish brown on the back, fading to white below. While most have one distinctive black spot at the base of the tail, some may have as many as a half dozen inside of yellow circles on each side. The body is elongated and thick, with a gently arched back and two dorsal fins. A three year old red drum typically weighs six to eight pounds.

WHERE AND WHEN: Redfish prefer to feed in shallow waters along the edges of bays and submerged vegetation. They relate to soft mud or sandy bottoms along jetties, pier pilings and jetties, and during cold spells, they can be found in tidal rivers and creeks. Most are caught in our Southern waters, well below Long Beach Island. The most productive season for reds is early summer.

BAIT AND TACKLE: Since red drum are primarily scent feeders, there is little disadvantage to using heavier line, especially in discolored or deeper water. Heavy bait casting tackle with strong braided line and leader is a good choice. Reds feed mainly on crustaceans, mollusks, squid and fishes and their favorite may well be shrimp. In coastal regions in the southernmost parts of the state, anglers armed with spinning gear bounce plastic jigs along the bottom in protected waters of bays and rivers and saltwater flycasters sight cast small surface popping plugs, baitfish type streamers or shrimp imitation flies to cruising reds.

STATE RECORD: The heaviest red drum taken in New Jersey was the 55 pound redfish that Daniel Yanion caught in Great Bay in 1985.

FOOD VALUE: Red drum have a moderate flavor and are not oily. Larger fish are tough and chewy, but smaller reds (under 15 pounds) are quite tasty, indistinguishable from black drum in flavor. One especially popular recipe is Cajun-style blackened redfish. ■

Eel, Conger

The Conger, unlike its cousin the American Eel, spends its life in salt water. The conger, also known as pout, is a true eel, with a continuous vertical fin and no fin spines. When they migrate hundreds of miles offshore to spawn, at about 15 years of age, they cease to eat, their heads change shape, their teeth fall out and their bones turn into jelly. The females release up to five million eggs each, the males fertilize the eggs and both adults die.

DESCRIPTION: Conger eels are distinguished from American eels largely by the mouth. The conger has an overbite, the upper jaw being longer than the lower. That condition is reversed in the American. In addition, the conger has a sharp projection protruding from its dorsal fin which can injure a careless angler. The adult conger's color is bluish-green but the color pales as they age.

WHERE AND WHEN: The conger is a bottom fish but it may be found in water of any depth, from a few inches to hundreds of feet. Congers have exceptionally large appetites and feed on fish, crabs, shrimp and small mollusks. They swim with ling and cod and are primarily caught in New Jersey waters in winter. Although they are thought to be largely nocturnal, congers are caught during daylight hours as well as at night.

BAIT AND TACKLE: Congers are most often caught by anglers targeting other bottom feeding species offshore. They are occasionally found in the mouths of saltwater rivers and bays, and once hooked, they fight surprisingly well. Light tackle and small hooks with bits of cut bait are how most are caught.

STATE RECORD: There is no current state record for conger eels.

FOOD VALUE: The conger has been placed on the "no retention, no harvest" list by NOAA in 2012, so food value is not an issue. ■

Fluke

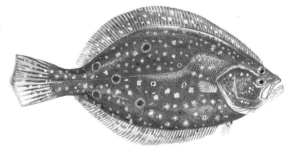

Fluke are one of the top three fish taken by New Jersey saltwater anglers each year, with a recreational harvest estimated in a recent year to be in excess of 1.7 million fish. They also are among the most important finfish in New Jersey's commercial fishery. As with other desirable species, size, bag and seasonal regulations are in place and change from season to season.

DESCRIPTION: The fluke is a flatfish with both eyes on the upper surface of the head when the fish is facing left. They have a remarkable ability to change color to match the bottom on which they are found. They are white below and dark above, where they can turn various shades of gray, brown, blue and almost black. The quickest differentiation of a fluke from a winter flounder is teeth. If it has teeth, it's a fluke.

WHERE AND WHEN: Fluke are primarily available to anglers in the summer months; hence their other common name, summer flounder. The season begins inshore, in protected waters which warm up more quickly than the ocean does. During these warmer months, they are widely distributed in near-shore coastal waters and bays throughout the state, including hotspots like Sandy Hook, Raritan Bay, Delaware Bay, Barnegat Bay and Elberon. Summer flounder bury themselves in the sand and change their back color to match the environment as they lie in wait for prey. Note: a less often sighted cousin of the fluke is the sundial.

On average, it is smaller and much thinner than a fluke, but also quite tasty.

BAIT AND TACKLE: Styles and equipment used to catch fluke continue to evolve. At one time a plain golden "Kahle" style hook in size 1/0 or 2/0, baited with a strip of squid and weighted to bounce along bottom, was typical. Today, a variety of artificials tipped with bait are used. For example, heavy round bucktail jigs or "Spro" jigs are worked at bottom, often "sweetened" with a strip of squid or mackerel. Inland, very light tackle and sinkers as light as one ounce add to the excitement of fluke fishing. Offshore, however, and most especially when a strong tide is running, a heavy boat rod and plenty of weight may be needed to stay at bottom, where 95% of the fluke are caught. Of note: larger 4/0 or 6/0 hooks are often recommended to reduce the chance that sub-legal fish might swallow the hook and be damaged or killed.

STATE RECORD: The heaviest fluke on record in the Garden State weighed 19 pounds 12 ounces and was caught off Cape May by Walter Lubin.

FOOD VALUE: Fluke are among our best tasting fish, with very white meat. Fluke may be at their best when stuffed with crab meat, a familiar recipe in good seafood restaurants. ■

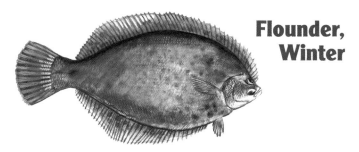

Flounder, Winter

The flounder is a flatfish species, characterized – as are fluke – by both eyes situated on the same side of its head. The larval flounder has eyes normally positioned but one eye migrates to the other side of the body in the course of early development. While winter flounder were once plentiful in our salt water rivers and bays, stocks have dropped precipitously because of overfishing, often with "fyke" nets, and pollution. Significantly, world stocks of flounder were estimated in 2003 to be only about 10% of pre-industrial levels.

DESCRIPTION: The upper side of the flounder is a dull brown while the lower side is white. Flounders are masters of camouflage, able to change coloration and even patterning to match the sand or mud bottom where they lie in wait for prey. Flounder are ambush predators, often covering themselves with a thin layer of sand to enhance camouflage as they hunt for worms and grass shrimp.

WHERE AND WHEN: In years past, our tastiest flounder were taken in November and December after the fish migrated from their offshore feeding grounds. Today, however, the numbers are so sharply diminished that fishing is limited to six or so weeks each spring. Modest catches of flounder are reported inshore, but as rivers and bays warm up, our "flatties" head offshore for deeper waters. Some of the largest flounder are caught out of season and released by anglers on headboats targeting ling and seabass.

BAIT AND TACKLE: In quiet water, very light spinning tackle with six to eight pound monofilament line and very small hooks are recommended. (Only if the tide is running is somewhat heavier tackle indicated.) Many anglers seem to prefer the old "Chesterton" style hook, but a size eight or size ten non-offset hook is best, especially since the smaller shank can be concealed in the bait. Preferred baits are a bit of yellow "sedge" mussel, a strip of skimmer clam tongue (filleted in half and tenderized by a sinker) or a piece of sand or blood worm with head removed.

STATE RECORD: Angler Jimmy Swanson caught the five pound 11 ounce state record winter flounder off of Barnegat Light in 1993.

FOOD VALUE: Flounder provide fine dining, plain and simple. ■

Hake, White

The white hake is a fast-growing species that is exceptionally fertile, with a single female producing several million eggs each spawning.

DESCRIPTION: Significantly, the white hake isn't white at all; rather, they are bronze or golden on the sides and yellow-white on the belly, with tiny black spots and muddy-colored fins. They are typically fat and homely, with an elongated body and threadlike fins extending from pelvic fins past the ends of the pectoral fin.

WHERE AND WHEN: White hake are often found around deep water wrecks. In general, they tend to be found wherever cod and pollock are located, and are often caught when these other species are targeted. Adult white hake eat large quantities of smaller fish and crustaceans. Winter is the most productive season for taking them.

BAIT AND TACKLE: In general, whatever gear is used for cod fishing is quite sufficient for white hake. A two hook rig, one tied above and one below a heavy sinker, is recommended. If targeting white hake, smaller hooks are recommended. Sizes 3/0 to 5/0 are adequate and also can hold a cod or pollock. Skimmer clam is the preferred bait but a chunk of herring also will induce bites.

STATE RECORD: Wayne Eble, a very famous surname down in Barnegat Light, holds the record for his 41 pound 7 ounce white hake.

He boated the beast in 1989.

FOOD VALUE: Despite its unlovely appearance, white hake is excellent table fare, whether fried, broiled or baked. Of note: the fish should be cleaned quickly to avoid spoiling of the fish's often significant stomach contents. ■

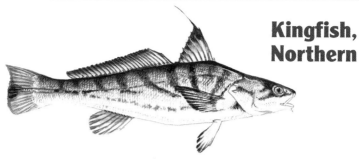

Kingfish, Northern

The northern kingfish is part of the drum family; however, since they lack an air bladder, they do not make typical drumming sounds like other family members. A migratory fish, the northern kingfish – also commonly referred to as northern whiting – regularly ply New Jersey waters from late April to October.

DESCRIPTION: Northern kingfish seldom exceed a pound in size. Dark in color, they range from black to brownish, with dark irregular bars along the body and downward facing mouths for bottom feeding. One notable characteristic is a long spine on the first dorsal fin. The bold markings and a dark stripe behind the pectoral fin distinguish it from the two other species of kingfish. Commonly these fish range from 10 to 14 inches in length.

WHERE AND WHEN: The northern kingfish is virtually never caught more than a mile off the beach. Most are caught by surfcasters or boats close to shore, from Cape May all the way up to Raritan Bay. River and bay anglers catch them in early fall around jetties, especially at low tide change. Kingfish also are taken by surf casters from late spring through early autumn. There are no bag or size limits on this species but very small fish are normally released.

BAIT AND TACKLE: Spinning gear is well suited to these smallish fish, equipped with ten pound test line and small hooks baited with blood worm, clam or even bits of super market shrimp. A high-low rig with size four bait holder

hooks is most productive. In the surf, a pyramid sinker is needed to keep your bait at bottom.

STATE RECORD: Chester Urbanski caught the state record northern kingfish in Barnegat Bay in 2004. It weighed 2 pounds 8 ounces.

FOOD VALUE: Larger northern kingfish are easy to fillet and make for a good meal, especially when deep fat fried quickly on a high heat. ■

Ling / Red Hake

The red hake, a close relative of the codfish, is considered a key mainstay of New Jersey's wintertime fishery these days. More commonly called ling, the world record was caught off New Jersey in 2010.

DESCRIPTION: The ling is easily identified by its pelvic fins, which are formed into long white streamers. The elongated body is variable in color, reddish brown to olive on the upper side, with lower skin and belly trending from dirty white to bright white.

WHERE AND WHEN: Big ling are plentiful the entire length of the Jersey coast in the winter months. Cold water is key, although ling also are taken in spring and early fall and even in summer in the 250 ft. deep water of "The Mudhole." Like most bottom feeders, ling prefer hard bottom, preferably near structure. They feed on crustaceans, rock crabs and small fish.

Three other members of the hake/codfish family are caught by New Jersey anglers but in very small numbers that do not justify entries in the state records. Still they bear mention here. The first is the silver hake, better known as the whiting or frost fish. As recently as the 1980s, our waters teemed with whiting but overfishing has reduced their numbers to a virtual handful. Second is the spotted hake, which resembles the red hake except for its spots and its size — seldom approaching the red. Third is the tommy cod, a fish that is a different species from a codfish and seldom approaches a pound in size.

BAIT AND TACKLE: If big fish are not present, red hake can be caught on heavy duty bait casting gear with line as light as 20 lb. test. If permitted, braided line is the best option to feel the bite. A basic bottom rig will suffice. A productive approach is a high low rig with 1/0 to 2/0 snelled beak-style hooks attached with dropper loops, one above and one below a bank sinker that is heavy enough to hold bottom. A piece of clam is most commonly used to attract ling. Chunks of herring or mackerel also produce strikes.

STATE RECORD: Billy Watson, an angler from Lansdale, Pa., caught the state and IGFA world record red hake 20 miles ESE of Manasquan NJ in February 2010. His record fish weighed a remarkable 12 pounds 13 ounces.

FOOD VALUE: It is difficult to find a fish that is more delicious than ling if properly handled. Especially in summer, they should be placed in a cooler filled with ice immediately upon being caught and then filleted on the boat to preserve their superb flavor. ■

Mackerel, Atlantic

Atlantic Mackerel, a/k/a "Boston Mackerel," are wonderful fighters that double as superb bait for other species. Mackerel are a fast swimming, schooling fish with a marked preference for cool, well-oxygenated open ocean waters. They feed largely on small fish, fry and fish eggs.

IDENTIFICATION: "Bostons" are striking in appearance. They are bright silver below the lateral line, with dark vertical lines upwards from the lateral on a blue-green body. The coloration is brilliant in the water but fades somewhat after fish are boated. Their smaller cousins, called "tinker" or "chub" mackerel, don't have stripes but instead are lightly spotted.

WHERE AND WHEN: Winter brings Atlantic mackerel to our waters in numbers that vary sharply from year to year. They are essentially a "feast or famine" fish, sometimes appearing in massive schools but often remaining largely absent. Unpredictable, too, is the length of time they stay around and how closely they come to our shores. Season in and season out, however, the Mudhole is among the best of all places to find them.

BAIT AND TACKLE: Once fish are located, heavy Diamond or Ava-style jigs are generally used in combination with two or three red teaser-type lures or tube jigs on a "tree," and it is not uncommon to catch two or three fish at a time. Fishing the right depth is critical to success. The most productive way to determine depth is dropping the jig to bottom and working it back up the water column in increments until fish are located.

STATE RECORD: The state record "Boston" weighed four pounds one ounce. It was caught by Abe Elkin at the Manasquan Ridge in 1983.

FOOD VALUE: Atlantic mackerel are prized as table fare by diners who enjoy fish with strong flavor. Its reddish flesh is firm textured and is known to promote good health, since it has an abundance of protein and vitamins and twice as much omega 3 as salmon. As a side note, filleted strips are top menu items for fluke and ling. Codfish, sharks and tuna are irresistibly attracted to slabs and even to whole mackerel. ■

Mackerel, King

King mackerel are prized by anglers for their powerful, blistering runs at speeds equaling their distant cousin, the wahoo. Although they are not commonly found in Jersey waters, their fighting ability, exceptional speed and presence in our record books earns them a place in this guide.

DESCRIPTION: The king is long and lean, with dark coloration on the back fading to bright silver on the sides and white on the belly. Its teeth, very similar to those of a bluefish, are large, closely spaced and razor sharp, dictating special care in handling and hook removal. Of note: a party boat owner recently required more than twenty stitches in his hand to close a slash from a king he was removing from a customer's hook.

WHERE AND WHEN: Kings are basically a subtropical species found in numbers well to our South. Most kings taken in New Jersey are found from Cape May to as far north as Atlantic County. Summer is the season for kings as warmer ocean currents bring a few to our offshore canyons. Size and bag limits are regulated.

BAIT AND TACKLE: A whole Spanish sardine is a meal of choice for kings. Trolling spoons, jigs and live bait produce kings as well. When trolling live bait, two joined hooks are typically tied to a strong metal leader, the first hooked through the bait fish's mouth and the second through the fish's back or allowed to swing

free. This responds to the king mackerel's tendency to bite the tail section of the bait fish. Most trollers use ocean outfits with at least 30 pound test line. Casters try for kings with level wind and spinning outfits and even fly rods at their own peril, given the long, sizzling runs of a hooked king.

STATE RECORD: It was off Cape May that angler Fernando Alfaiate took his record 54 pound king in 1998.

FOOD VALUE: The flesh of the king is rich and oily and is usually cut into steaks and broiled, grilled or smoked. As with other oily fish, kings are an acquired taste. ■

Mackerel, Spanish & Cero

Spanish and cero mackerel appear much less frequently in New Jersey waters than kings and resemble each other in many ways. They both are spirited fighters and more than welcomed additions to the near coastal fisheries. Note: ceros are even less frequently caught in New Jersey waters than Spanish or Kings.

DESCRIPTION: Spanish mackerel are beautifully colored finfish. Their slender bodies are blue and silver, spotted with golden yellow spots end to end. They are distinguished from the Cero or King Mackerel in having these spots without stripes on the sides and in lacking scales on the pectoral fins. The cero has a broken yellowish line that runs vertically from pectoral fin to tail. Characteristically cero also are larger than Spanish mackerel, often weighing 10 pounds or more, whereas Spanish average two to four pounds.

WHERE AND WHEN: Mackerel generally occur in our waters as transients. They are most often caught offshore in summer in South Jersey waters, usually from party and charter boats working within ten miles of land. In late summer these mackerel migrate southward to spend the winter and early spring.

BAIT AND TACKLE: Recreational anglers catch mackerel from boats while trolling wired feather lures in bright colors and by casting spoons, jigs and live bait. Speedy retrieves are key to catching these exceptionally fast swim-ming fish. Size and bag limits are in place. Of note: the management of the mackerel fishery is considered a success, since their numbers are on the rise today after years in decline.

STATE RECORD: As with their cousin the king mackerel, the top Spanish mackerel came from the waters off of Cape May. Donald Krenick boated his record 9 pound 12 ounce fish in 1990.

FOOD VALUE: Many people consider Spanish mackerel to be quite delicious, and certainly healthy. The darker meat of the Spanish is one of the richest sources for Omega 3 fatty acids. They are easily filleted and make excellent table fare whether smoked, poached, baked, broiled, steamed or fried. ■

Marlin, Blue

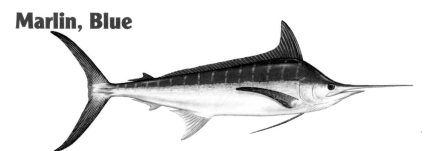

The blue marlin is considered by many to be the pinnacle of offshore big game fishing. The power and majesty of this great fish were immortalized in Ernest Hemingway's epic novella, "The Old Man and the Sea." Growing to almost unimaginable size and capable of spectacular fighting ability, these great fish make acrobatic jumps and sizzling dives to deep water in the course of exhausting yet exhilarating fights.

DESCRIPTION: The blue marlin is cobalt blue trending downward to a silver belly, often with quite vivid blue stripes that run vertically from back to belly. The jaw is elongated in the shape of a spear, and its dorsal, pectoral and anal fins are sharply pointed. Of course, sheer size and power are good indicators when the blue is first hooked.

WHERE AND WHEN: Blue marlin follow warming water temperatures and food stocks north as spring turns into summer. August and September are peak months for these great fish off the Jersey coast, and the deepwater canyons 100 miles or so out to sea are where they almost invariably are found. Blue marlin often migrate remarkable distances. For example, one fish tagged in the western Atlantic was re-caught in the Indian Ocean off the island of Mauritius.

BAIT AND TACKLE: Trolling is the style used to hook blue marlin, and the biggest and gaudiest of lures work best. The splash, bubble trail and action of well presented artificials attract the marlin's attention, and significantly, the lure almost can't be too large. (Of note: a yellowfin tuna weighing 155 pounds was found in the belly of the largest recorded blue marlin capture on hook and line, a 1,805 pound Pacific blue.) Only the heaviest and best rods, reels and lines are used in this larger-than-life sport, Lures and rigged natural baits are usually trolled at 7.5 to 9 knots, allowing substantial areas to be effectively worked in a day's fishing. Live bait trolling proceeds more slowly to keep the bait alive.

STATE RECORD: The New Jersey state record blue marlin weighed 1,046 pounds. Phil Infantolino was fishing in the Hudson Canyon in 1986 when he caught this monster fish — the heaviest fish of any kind ever caught in our waters.

FOOD VALUE: Blue Marlin are almost always released to fight another day. Since lures may weigh several pounds, lure removal by the mate — when the fish is sufficiently gassed — is preferred to cutting the line in the release process. ■

Marlin, White

The white marlin, although characteristically much smaller than the blue, is nonetheless a great sport fish, capable of powerful runs and wild leaps. They are more populous in our waters than their larger cousins – by a margin of 15 to one in some estimates. They are known to use their long sword-like bills to stun fast moving fish, which they then turn to consume.

DESCRIPTION: The white marlin is a truly beautiful species, with coloration that is blue to chocolate brown on top, shading to a silvery white belly. Faint white stripes traverse the fish vertically, and the tips of the dorsal, pectoral and first anal fin are rounded. The upper jaw forms a spear.

WHERE AND WHEN: Like their larger cousins, white marlin migrate northward in late spring and summer, following water temperatures and prey items, including a wide variety of fish, squid and crustaceans. Beginning in June, experienced big game anglers start looking for the first whites to appear. The fish are found on the edge of the continental shelf, some 80 to 100 miles offshore, better known as "The Canyons." The preferred habitat for white marlin is 300 feet or deeper in the southern canyons off South Jersey, where the bite reportedly has been superb the past several summers.

BAIT AND TACKLE: Since white marlin average 45 to 65 pounds in size, lighter rods, reels and lines can be used. Boats targeting whites switch to 30 pound set-ups and troll natural baits, including naked ballyhoo and big strips of false albacore or other oily fish. Characteristically lines are rigged with circle hooks so that fish can be released without damage. Of course, targeting white marlin is a problem, since any number of larger and more powerful game fish share the same water column.

STATE RECORD: The state record white marlin was taken at the Hudson Canyon in 1980 by Mike Marchell. His fish weighed 137 pounds 8 ounces.

FOOD VALUE: Prevailing laws dictate that most billfish be released. Consequently food value is not a consideration when white marlin are taken. ■

Perch, White

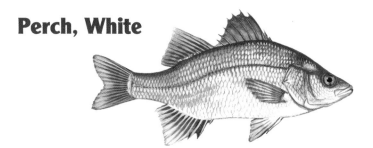

White perch are equally at home in salt and fresh water, and in fact resemble their larger cousins, the striped bass, which live in the ocean but head inland into rivers to spawn. Some, it should be noted, are entirely land-locked in impoundments and lakes. Whether caught in salt water or fresh, they are plentiful, scrappy and delicious, and thus have everything to recommend them to anglers.

DESCRIPTION: White perch are bright silver with dark backs, with one dark longitudinal line running along their bodies. On average, fully grown white perch range upwards of 12 inches long and weigh about one pound, although the salt water state record is nearly triple that weight. In some areas they are referred to as "blue nose" perch.

WHERE AND WHEN: White perch are widely distributed throughout the state's salt and fresh waters. The most productive environment for catching perch in numbers is brackish salt water, most especially creek mouths, dropoffs to deep water and eddies. They range from open water to obstructions such as bridges and rocky structure. They often appear in dense schools in early spring and fishing is especially active when a school is located.

During summer months perch are more widely dispersed. Most of New Jersey's tidal rivers offer fine perch fishing, including the Mullica, Bass, Raritan, Manasquan, Toms, Great Egg Harbor, Tuckahoe and Maurice Rivers. Late winter is most productive, especially through the ice in brackish water.

BAIT AND TACKLE: Ultra-lite spinning gear is fine in summer and spring but little ice fishing rods are best when fishing in dead of winter. Minnows, worms, grass shrimp and small live killies are the top live baits, and horizontal jigs or very small crappie lures are the most effective artificials.

STATE RECORD: The record white perch caught in salt water weighed 2 pounds 12 ounces when taken by Michael King in 1998 at Little Beach Creek. The fresh water record white perch, tipping the scales at 3 pounds one ounce, was caught in Forest Hill Lake by Edward Tango in 1989.

FOOD VALUE: Their white flesh is excellent, whether fried, broiled or baked. Anything over a half pound can be filleted, but smaller ones can be fried whole. ■

Pollock

The Pollock is part of a family of fish that includes cod, whiting, haddock and hake. A better fighter than the cod, the pollock is an aggressive fish that is as prized for the table as for its scrappiness.

DESCRIPTION: Pollock can grow to three feet or more in length. It has a strongly defined silvery lateral line with a greenish black hue above the stripe and a white underbelly.

WHERE AND WHEN: Pollock relate to rocky underwater terrain and structure, most especially shipwrecks in water as deep as 200 feet. Significantly most pollock are hooked from ten to twenty feet above the structure, often in the hours before daylight.

BAIT AND TACKLE: Stiff rods and big reels are a must because pollock can achieve great size and fight well. Jigging is the approach that most often produces strikes. Norwegian jigs with red plastic- tipped treble hooks often do best. Some anglers add a second treble above the jig. The lure is held well off bottom and jigged aggressively up and down, or dropped to bottom, reeled up 20 turns and quickly dropped back. Most often the Pollock will hit the jig as it is falling.

STATE RECORD: John Holton set the New Jersey state record in 1975 with his 46 pound 7 ounce fish caught off of Brielle. At the time, this fish also set an I.G.F.A. world record.

FOOD VALUE: Pollock is considered a "white fish" that is tasty and healthy to eat. Most of the fish served in fast food restaurants are pollock, a fact that reflects their availability to commercial fishermen well to our north as well as their attractiveness on the table. ■

Porgy

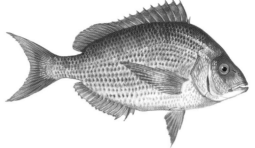

The porgy is among the most popularly sought fish in New Jersey salt water, and for good reason. They fight very well for their size, they are widely available, they are easily caught and they make for fine dining when cooked fresh. The primary species found locally are called "scup" in New England.

DESCRIPTION: Porgies have deep, oblong bodies, similar in shape to freshwater sunfish, that are silvery pink in color. They have a single dorsal fin and small mouths equipped with strong teeth that handle a diet of hard-shelled invertebrates and fish. Most do not exceed 15 inches in length and 2 pounds in weight, although occasionally they attain size of five pounds or more in New Jersey.

WHERE AND WHEN: Porgies relate to hard structure such as offshore wrecks and rock piles and are caught in depths ranging from 25 feet to as much as 200 feet. Summer is the most productive time for catching them.

BAIT AND TACKLE: When fishing offshore, bait-casting tackle with 20 pound test line is more than adequate unless a heavy tide is running. Two snelled hooks tied in tandem below a bank sinker large enough to hold bottom is the preferred style. Size two or size four offset baitholder hooks work well if the fish are running a pound or less in size. If they are running larger, a size 1/0 or 2/0 is recommended. Pieces of skimmer clam, strips of squid or bloodworms all work well as bait.

STATE RECORD: The state record porgy was caught in Delaware Bay in 1976 by Victor Rone. It weighed an impressive 5 pounds 14 ounces.

FOOD VALUE: White porgy fillets make fine dining. They can be pan fried, baked or broiled with equal gustatory success as long as the chef is careful not to overcook the main course. ■

Sailfish

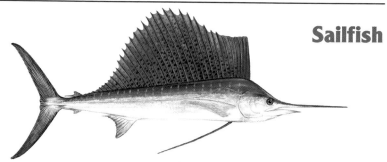

The sailfish is one of the most sought-after pelagic (fish that live near the surface) sport fish found off the entire east coast of the United States. Although smaller than its relatives, the marlin and the swordfish, this great billfish is especially known for its incredible jumps and sizzling speed, rivaled only by the wahoo at 68 m.p.h.

DESCRIPTION: The sailfish is the easiest of the bill fish to recognize because of its distinctive dorsal fin that looks like a sail. The first of the two dorsal fins, running most of the length of the body, is very long and tall, with the 20th ray the longest. The sail is folded and to the side when swimming but is raised when sailfish are hooked. Sails are predominantly blue to gray in color, often highlighted by stripes of iridescent blue and silver dots. They can change their colors almost instantly, rapidly turning its body light blue with yellowish stripes when excited.

WHERE AND WHEN: Sailfish also frequent Jersey's offshore canyons and normally feed high up in the water column. They are often seen at the surface, making sight casting a potentially wonderful experience.

BAIT AND TACKLE: Skilled anglers have taken sailfish on heavy spinning gear and salt water flyrods. In both cases, the reel must be of high quality with capacity to hold significant quantities of 20 pound test monofilament line. Traditionally most sailfishing has been done with rigged trolling baits such as Spanish sardines or ballyhoos. Since billfish often attack to stun or kill prey before circling back to swallow it, a good tactic is to drop back after one strikes at a trolled bait and free-spool the line so the fish will think it has injured the bait. Another technique is to lure the sails near the stern with live bait and then cast to them with a fly, which the sails often will attack instantly. Yet another method is trolling a live bait with a much more visually attractive artificial lure over it. The scent the baitfish puts in the water frequently attracts sailfish into going after the trolled lure.

STATE RECORD: Dr. John Tallia caught the state record sailfish, a fine 43 pound 3 ounce specimen, in 2006 at the Lindenkohl Canyon.

FOOD VALUE: Sailfish should be kept only when inadvertently killed, but otherwise released quickly and unharmed. If the angler wants a trophy, he has only to take measurements and a photograph before release. This great game fish is seldom thought of in terms of preparation for the table, especially since their meat is relatively tough. ■

Shad, Hickory & Gizzard

Of three shad specimens found in New Jersey, the American is by far the largest and most sought after, usually caught on migrations from saltwater up fresh water rivers to spawn. Consequently it is covered in our freshwater section. Hickory and gizzard shad are important in other contexts, most especially as forage fish for larger species and as bait.

DESCRIPTION: The gizzard shad has a silvery/bronze body and a dark blue black back, with dark stripes along its upper back. Like the hickory shad, it has a dark shoulder spot. The key identifier of the gizzard, however, is the long and thin filament formed by the last dorsal ray. The gizzard commonly grows to 14 inches in length. The hickory shad has a gray green back, a deep belly and a lower jaw that projects significantly past the upper jaw. It may grow up to 24 inches.

WHERE AND WHEN: Hickory shad may be caught wherever American shad are caught, in near-shore salt water and up saltwater rivers such as the Shark, Manasquan and Maurice. They arrive up rivers and are caught in early spring, usually just before the in-migrations of their larger cousins, the American shad. Gizzards live in a variety of open waters, both clear and silty, including rivers, swamps, lakes and bays, They have been witnessed in large schools near dams, warm water outlets and turbine outflows, and in freshwater impoundments such as the Manasquan Reservoir and Deal Lake. Of interest: gizzard shad are a preferred food of largemouth bass, and it is widely believed that bass fishing is best where gizzards are abundant. However, in some venues, gizzards grow quickly and become too large for most bass to swallow, so their value as a forage fish may be limited.

BAIT AND TACKLE: Sabiki rigs catch shad as do plain gold size 8 Kahle-style hooks tied in tandem, three in a line. However, since some shad stocks have been depleted, regulations are in place regarding which may be kept and which must be released.

STATE RECORD: Robert Macejka of Point Pleasant Beach reeled in the new state record hickory shad from the surf at Mantoloking in 2011. The fish weighed 2 pounds 13 ounces. There is no record for gizzard shad, since none has been caught that met the minimum weight requirement for a record fish.

FOOD VALUE: The hickory shad produces roe that is just as appealing to diners as American shad roe. ■

Sharks
In New Jersey

Sharks in Jersey waters? Absolutely. In fact, Peter Benchley's stunning novel and movie, "Jaws," was inspired by shark attacks that took place along the Jersey Shore almost a century ago: the first attack was off Beach Haven, the second off Spring Lake and the third in the backwaters of Raritan Bay. The great white shark that terrified millions of movie goers is an anomaly here today. The hammerhead, tiger, bull, dusky, sandbar/brown and porbeagle sharks are occasionally found in New Jersey waters. However, three species of sharks are quite common: the blue shark, the thresher shark and the shortfin mako.

A cautionary note: It is strongly advised that shark fishing be a charter boat experience, since the crew will have all of the safety and fishing equipment, the license and the knowledge required to subdue and land a shark safely. With many sharks weighing 100 pounds or more and all equipped with rows of razor sharp teeth, angling for them requires the help of experts.

Sharks, Blue

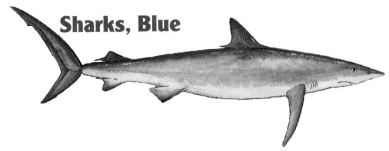

Blue sharks are migratory fish that inhabit deep water. They travel in schools and feed primarily on smaller fish and squid, although their diets may also include crab, small sharks, lobster, carrion and occasionally, sea birds. Because they hunt in packs, they are often referred to as "wolves of the sea." It is estimated that 10 to 20 million blue sharks are killed worldwide each year as a result of fishing.

DESCRIPTION: The blue shark has long pectoral fins and coloration of deep blue on top shading to lighter coloration of the sides and white belly. They tend to be somewhat lethargic but can achieve surprising speed when hooked.

WHERE AND WHEN: Blues prefer cooler water and are generally caught well down in the water column. Areas of deepwater wrecks like "The Mudhole" are ideal, as much as 30 miles offshore. Also, many are caught out in the Canyons by anglers hunting tuna. Occasionally, blues are taken closer in, hitting baits that are intended for bluefish or cod.

BAIT AND TACKLE: A long, uninterrupted chum slick is vital to shark fishing. Since blue sharks do not characteristically fight well for their size, lighter boat tackle and line as light as 20 pound test may suffice. A wire leader is requisite tackle.

STATE RECORD: The state record blue shark, tipping the scales at 366 pounds, was caught at "The Mud Hole" in 1996 by William Young Jr.

FOOD VALUE: Blue sharks are not widely sought for food, although the flesh is edible. ■

Sharks, Mako

Short fin mako sharks are beloved by sport fishermen everywhere for their powerful runs and extraordinary leaps. Scientists estimate that makos can leap 30 feet in the air and exceed 60 m.p.h. in bursts of speed that tear line off reels. They were celebrated in Ernest Hemingway's classic, "Old Man and the Sea," and in the writings of outdoor author Zane Gray, who was fascinated by the mako's menacing appearance and volatility. They are considered apex predators because they feed on the fastest and most well developed prey species like tunas. They also are responsible for 42 recorded attacks on humans between 1980 and 2010, three of which were fatal. Some hooked makos have been known to leap into boats, injuring passengers.

DESCRIPTION: Makos are streamlined and powerfully built, with large, well developed eyes and five large gill slits. They have striking coloration, with deep purple to indigo backs, silvery sides and white bellies. It is often said that among sharks, only blue sharks can rival makos for beautiful coloring.

WHERE AND WHEN: Rarely caught inshore, most mako sharks are Canyon dwellers. Makos feed throughout the water column and are as likely to take baits near the surface as hundreds of feet down. Late spring and summer are the most productive seasons for offshore angling for makos.

BAIT AND TACKLE: Heavy saltwater gear and a braided wire leader are necessities when fishing for these powerful, fast running sharks. Chumming with the bloodiest of fish – ground bunker or false albacore – will bring the fish within range. A live bluefish, rigged on a balloon float, may provide the best chance of a hookup, although fillets from bluefish, bonito or false albacore also will induce strikes.

STATE RECORD: Christopher Palmer caught the state record 856 pound mako at Wilmington Canyon in 1994.

FOOD VALUE: The flesh of the short fin mako makes excellent table fare. However, a consideration favoring release is the sharp decrease in their numbers worldwide. Hunted both by sport fishermen and commercial fishing operations, rapidly declining stocks give pause to keeping a mako for the table. ■

Sharks, Thresher

The thresher shark is immediately identified by its long scythe-like tail, which it employs in hunting schooling fish such as herring and mackerel. It slaps at schooling fish with this unique tail to stun and herd them closer together; then it attacks with open jaws.

DESCRIPTION: As noted, the most useful identifying characteristic of the thresher shark is its remarkable tail, which can be as long as the rest of its body. It has small jaws with small, curved teeth, and coloration varying from brown to black and irregular white markings on the underside.

WHERE AND WHEN: The thresher shark is a summer visitor to New Jersey and is most frequently caught in layers of deep offshore waters and areas of steep bottom contours. However, warmer water temperatures bring some threshers close to shore where they may be taken by surf casters equipped with strong surf rods. Threshers are caught in New Jersey waters throughout the summer and into early fall in a variety of habitats, from the deepest canyons far offshore to a few miles out in bluefish territory.

BAIT AND TACKLE: Threshers are known for their brute strength and endurance, with a reputation for burning drags and challenging anglers for hours. Consequently heavy stand-up gear with lots of line capacity is absolutely necessary for fishing offshore, with 100 pound test line, 10 to 15 foot braided wire leaders and a 9/0 hook recommended. Live bluefish are an attractive bait for these aggressive hunters, although many are caught on rigged sardines and huge chunks of cut bait.

STATE RECORD: The state record thresher, a 683 pound leviathan, was caught by Bennett Fogelberg while fishing "The Fingers" in 2009.

FOOD VALUE: The thresher, like the mako, is delicious table fare. However, anglers should consider that the thresher is on the Endangered Species list when deciding whether or not to release it back to the wild. ■

Sheepshead

The sheepshead is a member of the porgy family that commonly reaches 15 to 20 inches. Its diet consists of such hard items as clams, barnacles, fiddler crabs and oysters, and it has a hard mouth with several rows of strong teeth to crush the shells of its prey.

DESCRIPTION: The sheepshead has a deep and compressed body shape with 5 to 6 darker vertical bars on the silvery gray sides of the body. It has sharp and strong spines on dorsal and anal fins and prominent teeth, including incisors, molars and rounded grinders. The head in profile is oddly reminiscent of a sheep; thus its curious name. Most sheepshead caught are in the one to two pound range, but they are common to 8 pounds in some venues and may reach 20 pounds.

WHERE AND WHEN: Sheepshead arrive near shore in spring for spawning, gathering over and around rocky bottoms, debris, artificial reefs, piers, bridges and docks. They often are found in the brackish water of estuaries. They are primarily caught by bottom fishing hard bottom, wrecks, reefs, bridges and structure, usually in inshore waters south of Long Beach Island.

BAIT AND TACKLE: One hand spinning tackle and bait casting outfits with 12 pound test line and small hooks are sufficient to the task of taking sheepshead, which are notorious bait stealers. (This has prompted the observation that to catch sheepshead, anglers must strike before they bite!) Since sheepshead do not readily strike artificials, they are best fished for with live bait or cut natural baits, including shrimps, mussels, crab, worms, sand eels or mackerel strips. Occasionally sheepshead will strike a small ¼ ounce jig when it is cast into well-chummed waters where the fish are feeding.

STATE RECORD: The state record sheepshead, caught by Paul Lowe in Manahawkin Bay in 2003, weighed an impressive 17 pounds 3 ounces.

FOOD VALUE: Sheepshead are tasty when filleted and broiled. ■

Spot

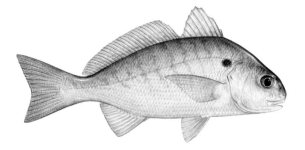

The spot, or spot croaker, once called a "Lafayette," is a popular salt water panfish found in shallower bays and estuaries during summer months and out in coastal waters when the temperature drops. They are bottom feeders mainly subsisting on worms, mollusks and small crustaceans, and are themselves an important prey species for striped bass, weakfish, summer flounder, bluefish and small sharks.

DESCRIPTION: The spot is a deep bodied flat fish, gray blue to golden yellow in color fading to yellow ventrally. The head is blunt with a small mouth. The most significant identifying mark and the source of its name is a large black spot set above the upper edge of the gill cover.

WHERE AND WHEN: As noted, spot are found inshore during warmer months of late spring, summer and early fall. Southern Jersey rivers and bays are notable for their spot populations, especially in the Delaware Bay area. However, spot also are found further north as waters warm. Cape May Point, Crow Shoal and the Cape Shore Channel are especially good fishing areas for this species. Spot can sometimes be caught in great numbers by recreational anglers from piers and anchored boats.

BAIT AND TACKLE: Since spot are quite small, the lightest spinning or baitcasting gear is fine, with small bits of squid or clam as bait, secured on a size 8 or size 10 hook.

STATE RECORD: The state record spot registered less than one pound on the scale. It weighed 13 ounces when Robert Belsky Jr. caught it in 2003 at Little Sheepshead Creek.

FOOD VALUE: Spot provide good table fare when fried whole. They are somewhat bony, though, and require a certain amount of work when eaten. It should be added that striped bass and doormat sized fluke have a particular appetite for spot, so smaller ones may be kept alive to use for bait. ■

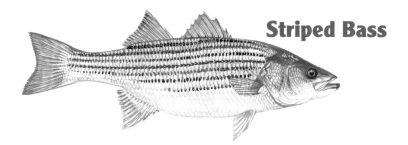

Striped Bass

The striped bass is a true conservation success story, thanks to programs put in place by the state in the 1980s. Stripers may be the single most widely sought game fish in New Jersey salt water due to their size, their powerful fighting ability and their availability close to shore. They migrate between salt and fresh water to spawn and can reach weights of 100 pounds or more.

DESCRIPTION: Stripers have streamlined silver bodies marked with horizontal dark stripes from gills to tail. They have large mouths with jaws hinging below the eye. They often are slim in appearance in spring but normally fatten up considerably by late summer after gorging on forage fish in saltwater bays and tidal rivers.

WHERE AND WHEN: Stripers usually arrive in mid to late April and stay around until well after Christmas. They roam the coast and are found in numbers in popular fishing venues like Raritan Bay, Sandy Hook Rip and Channel, Flynns Knoll, Roamer Shoal, Shrewsbury Rocks, Manasquan Inlet Jetty, Barnegat Inlet Jetties and along rock jetties on Long Beach Island and Delaware Bay. They winter over in tidal rivers like the Delaware, Raritan, Mullica and Maurice. (It should be noted that (1) it is always illegal to fish for stripers in Federal waters more than three miles offshore, and (2) size and bag limits are in place for legal waters.

BAIT AND TACKLE: Most anglers use heavy bait-casting tackle for stripers, although party boat gear is a safer bet to land the really large "cows." Drifting live eels or sandworms accounts for most hookups. Sandworms in the spring and eels in the fall is a good rule of thumb. Spring bass also are caught on fresh skimmer clam. When huge schools of menhaden ("bunker") appear, anglers switch to live-lining bunker as well as using bunker chunks, usually the entire head. Trolling jigs, spoons, plugs or umbrella rigs also produces plenty of strikes, especially when lures are worked close to bottom.

STATE RECORD: Until 2012, the New Jersey State record striper was also the world record. This 78 pound 8 ounce bruiser was caught while fishing on an Atlantic City Jetty by Al McReynolds in 1982. The freshwater record striper, weighing in at 51 pounds even, was caught by John Christian in 2002 in the Great Egg Harbor River.

FOOD VALUE: The striped bass is a delicious fish, especially when the dark layer under the skin is filleted away. It has a firm texture, moist white meat and mild flavor that make for real dining pleasure. ■

Swordfish

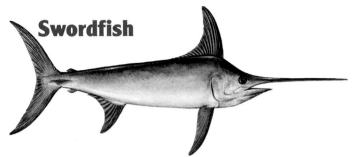

Swordfish are vigorous, powerful fighters that prowl the New Jersey canyons, challenging the skill, tackle and endurance of offshore anglers. It is undoubtedly one of the fastest fish in the sea, capable of speeds estimated by some of 60 m.p.h. When hooked, some have been known to dive so quickly that they impale their swords into the ocean bottom.

DESCRIPTION: The color of this great fish's back is variable from black to grayish blue to brown to metallic purple, the remainder a bright white. Its upper jaw is long, flat and sword-like, and it is known to utilize its sword not to impale prey, but to slash at and stun them. Swordfish once averaged 200 pounds, but overharvesting has reduced the average size of commercially caught fish quite considerably. However, they are rebounding fairly well today, both in size and in numbers.

WHERE AND WHEN: The New Jersey swordfish grounds are 70 to 80 miles offshore in the canyons on the edge of the continental shelf. Charter boat captains fish the 100 fathom curve drifting in 600 to 1200 feet of water. Although swords are known to frequent depths of 400 to 500 fathoms, they occasionally are seen basking at the surface.

Swordfishing season begins in July and continues through early fall, and nighttime is almost always better than daytime for finding and taking swords.

BAIT AND TACKLE: Stand-up rod/reel combinations are necessary, and the best baits are live squid and mackerel. Large chunks of mackerel, herring, mullet, bonito or squid also produce results, and since most fishing is done in dark of night, specialized plastic glow sticks often are attached to attract fish.

STATE RECORD: The state record for swordfish is long standing. The 530 pound record fish was caught in 1964 by Edmund Levitt, fishing Wilmington Canyon.

FOOD VALUE: Swordfish is a particularly popular fish for cooking. The flesh is firm and can be cooked in ways more fragile types of fish cannot (e.g., over a grill on skewers.) In 1998, overfishing by commercial long liners led to a national campaign asserting that swordfish numbers were endangered by their popularity as a restaurant entree. Subsequently President Bill Clinton called for a ban on the sale and import of swordfish, and the federal government placed 132,670 square miles of the Atlantic Ocean off limits to swordfishing. Moreover, the FDA recommends that young children, pregnant women and women of childbearing age not eat swordfish because of potential toxicity from high levels of mercury that accumulates in the flesh of these top-of-the-line predators. ■

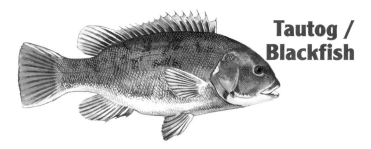

Tautog / Blackfish

Blackfish also are commonly called "tautog," "tog" or "slippery bass." That last name connotes the protective coating of slime that covers them. They are long lived and slow growing.

DESCRIPTION: Blackish brown in color, blackfish are stumpy in stature, squat in appearance and rather homely. However, because of their surging power when hooked, a ten pound tog may appear quite beautiful to the lucky angler who boats him.

WHERE AND WHEN: Blackfish relate to structure and are found in a variety of environments, from rocky ledges in relatively shallower water to deep water wrecks and artificial reef sites down 150 feet or more. As to bag limits and seasons when blackfish may be kept, the angler should carefully consult regulations in the current Saltwater Digest published by the New Jersey Division of Fish and Wildlife.

BAIT AND TACKLE: Because "tog" are caught in structure, a stiff-action rod is a must, with conventional reels and braided line when allowed. Size 3 or 4 "Virginia" hooks are commonly used, often rigged singly to be sure a second hook doesn't grab part of the wreck. Some anglers use two hooks, often putting both barbs into the same bait, especially if baiting with a small green crab. Crabs and pieces of conch are the most effective baits.

STATE RECORD: The largest tautog taken in New Jersey was boated off Ocean City in 1998 by Anthony Monica. It weighed 25 pounds and is thought to be the World Record for the species.

FOOD VALUE: Scaling is nearly impossible but a blackfish can be filleted and skinned with ease. Tog can be served baked or broiled to good effect and cooking them in a fish chowder produces wonderful results. ■

Tilefish

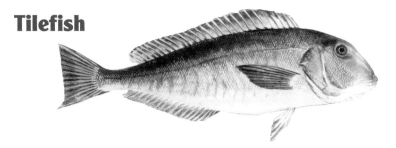

Two species of tilefish, the golden and the blueline or gray, hunt in the deep waters off New Jersey, and since their numbers are limited, they will be treated together here.

DESCRIPTION: The golden tilefish is quite colorful, with a blue-green back that fades to a pearly white belly. It is touched with red and blue iridescence, highlighted by irregular yellow-gold spots. The blueline tilefish is considerably less colorful, gray in color with a few blue parallel lines from face to body.

WHERE AND WHEN: Tilefish are shelter-seeking fish, habituating vertical and horizontal burrows in the clay and silt substrates of the upper slopes and flanks of offshore submarine canyons. The tilefish are considered important modifiers of habitat on the outer continental shelf because of the frequency and density of their burrowing activity. They are found in depths no less than 350 feet and anglers often fish for them at twice that depth. The prime season is late spring through mid fall, with many boats targeting tilefish along with tuna.

BAIT AND TACKLE: Heavy gear, braided line and big reels are absolutely requisite for this deep water fishing. Drifting for tilefish requires ultra heavy sinkers, in the five to ten pound class. Common sash weights are often used. Electric reels sometimes are employed because reeling up such heavy weight from so great a depth is exhausting. Size 6/0 hooks are commonly used, either in one or two hook rigs,

and whole squid are the recommended bait, not least because they stay on the hook well.

STATE RECORD: The heaviest golden tilefish weighed 63 pounds 8 ounces and was caught in the Lindenkohl Canyon by Dennis Muhlenforth in 2009. The state record blueline tilefish weighed 18 pounds 7 ounces and was boated by Joseph Sanzone at Tom's Canyon in 2007.

FOOD VALUE: Incredible! The firm, white meat of the golden is mildly flavored and extra lean, and is often called a poor man's lobster. The bluelines are very good too, but not quite the quality of the golden. ■

Triggerfish

Triggerfish are widely distributed throughout the Atlantic, from Massachusetts to Brazil. This hardy fish, shaped much like a porgy, derives its name from its first dorsal spine, which normally rests in a groove but when erect remains up until the smaller second spine is deflexed, triggering the first.

DESCRIPTION: The triggerfish, gray in color with faint vertical bands, has an oval shaped, highly compressed body. The head is large and features a small but strong-jawed mouth with teeth adapted for crushing shells. It feeds largely on bottom dwelling crustaceans, mollusks and barnacles. It uses its strong jaws and teeth to dislodge and crush mussels. The skin of the triggerfish is inordinately tough, making filleting a challenge without a strong and very sharp knife.

WHERE AND WHEN: Triggerfish reach New Jersey waters in early summer and are found at many of the same wrecks and other hard bottom structure where porgies are found. Many head inshore and are caught at jetties and piers, especially in South Jersey.

BAIT AND TACKLE: Triggerfish are notorious bait stealers. Rather than ingesting a whole bait, they nibble off small bites. Thus smaller, tougher baits, rigged on sharp #2 or # 4 hooks, are recommended. Light party boat rods and reels are more than sufficient to the task; indeed, bait casting outfits with 20 pound test line are better yet. (Note: the same teeth that crush barnacles with ease can render a nasty bite, so anglers should exercise care in removing hooks.)

STATE RECORD: The state record triggerfish weighed 5 pounds 12 ounces. It was caught by Ronald Pires at High Bar Harbor in 2008.

FOOD VALUE: Truly excellent as table fare. When served in restaurants, it most often is shown as "turbot" on the menu. Note: a pinkish filament lies under the dorsal and anal fins and has a slightly bitter taste, so care should be exercised to fillet it away. The remainder of the flesh is bone-free and nearly pure white. ■

Tuna, Albacore

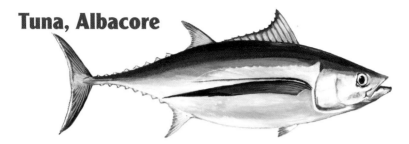

The albacore tuna is one of the most commonly hunted tuna species in the world, not least because of its well deserved reputation as a battler. Also called "long-fin" tuna, albacore tuna migrate around the world and prey upon smaller tuna, mackerel and other pelagic species.

DESCRIPTION: The albacore is the easiest of the tunas to identify because of their extra long pectoral fins and the white trailing edge of the tail. They characteristically weigh between 10 and 50 pounds, although fully grown adults can run a bit larger.

WHERE AND WHEN: As with most tuna, the canyons off the coast of New Jersey are prime hunting grounds for albacore tuna, especially at color or temperature breaks. These fishing grounds, located on the edge of the continental shelf, are 75 to 100 miles out to sea. The classic tuna hunting ground is the Hudson Canyon, the largest and most northern canyon in the state, which lies about 70 miles due east of the Manasquan Inlet. Water temperatures and drop-offs are perfectly conducive to prey species attractive to tuna as the Gulf Stream's warm water eddies well up along the canyon walls and the water at the canyon tip drops from 200 feet down to 600 feet. The season for fishing the canyons is late June through early October.

BAIT AND TACKLE: Stand-up trolling gear is recommended, with multiple lines worked off of out riggers. Each line is generally baited with a rigged ballyhoo, Spanish sardine or fresh squid. Albacore also are taken on lures. Skirted ballyhoo, Islander, spreader bar or green machine are popular choices.

STATE RECORD: The state record albacore tuna was taken at the Spencer Canyon by Dr. S. Scannapiego in 1984. It weighed 77 pounds 15 ounces.

FOOD VALUE: Albacore tuna has a firm, beefsteak-type texture, with large flakes and a mild rich taste. It is much lighter in color that yellowfin or bluefin, and devotees of grilled tuna usually love albacore, especially when served rare. ■

Tuna, Bluefin

The bluefin tuna, which has been hunted by mankind for thousands of years, is the largest of the tuna species, sometimes exceeding 1,000 pounds. They can dive to depths of more than 3,000 feet and reach speeds of 40 miles per hour as they hunt such typical prey species as sardines, herring, mackerel and squid.

DESCRIPTION: The body of the bluefin is dark blue above and gray below, with gold sparkles marking the body and bright yellow tail finlets adding to the coloration. The top part of the dorsal fin has a dark blue edge, unlike other tuna.

WHERE AND WHEN: Some bluefins are hooked closer to shore than might be imagined, given their size. Consequently, while the canyons are a good bet for bluefin trolling, some are caught as close in as the Mud Hole, little more than a dozen miles from land. Summer is the prime season, but some bluefins are caught in spring and fall.

BAIT AND TACKLE: Very heavy gear is an absolute necessity when the quarry is bluefin, with line testing to 100 pounds or more. Offshore, many of the biggest fish are caught by trolling, especially around warm water temperature breaks and changes in water color. Boats troll large plugs or carefully rigged whole ballyhoo. (Note: breaking off the ballyhoo's beak causes it to move in a more lifelike fashion.) When fishing the Mud Hole and other spots closer in, chumming with bunker and using live bunker, ling or bluefish may very well induce a lurking bluefin to strike.

STATE RECORD: The state record bluefin tuna weighted a staggering 1,030 pounds 6 ounces when caught by Royal Parson off Point Pleasant in 1981.

FOOD VALUE: The bluefin is one of the most highly prized fish used in Japanese raw fish dishes. About 80% of all Atlantic bluefin tunas are consumed on that small island nation, where one bluefin caught off our eastern shoreline several years ago sold for $15,400. Not surprisingly, the Japanese appetite for sushi and the consequent high prices paid for fish are major threats to the wild stocks of our Atlantic bluefin. It is fortunate that serious restrictions have now been placed on their capture and retention here. ■

Tuna, Skipjack

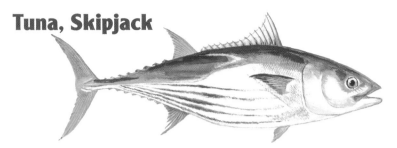

The skipjack is the tuna least often caught in New Jersey waters. However, the lucky light-tackle angler who manages to hook one has a superb fight on his hands.

DESCRIPTION: The skipjack is similar in appearance to false albacore, with a dark blue back and silver flank and belly. What distinguishes the "skippie" is a series of four to six horizontal-diagonal stripes along its upper sides, whereas the false albacore's stripes start behind the pectoral fin. It commonly weighs two to ten pounds.

WHERE AND WHEN: Skipjacks relate to warmer water and are most often found in the southern canyons offshore of Atlantic and Cape May Counties. Summer is the season.

BAIT AND TACKLE: One hand spinning and bait casting rigs are well suited to fishing for skipjack, whether trolling or casting small feather lures and spoons. Some "skippies" are hooked by "squidding" Ava-style jigs, casting well away from the boat, allowing the jig to drop to bottom and then reeling quickly, stopping at intervals for a second or two. This often induces a bite, not only from a lurking skipjack but also from a bluefish, bonito or false albacore.

STATE RECORD: The largest skipjack on record in New Jersey weighed 13 pounds 4 ounces. This state record fish was caught by Craig Eberbach out in the Wilmington Canyon in 1999.

FOOD VALUE: Although the skipjack is sold fresh, frozen, canned, dried, salted and smoked in other countries, it is not usually sought as a table fish in the United States. The flesh is oily and very strongly flavored. ■

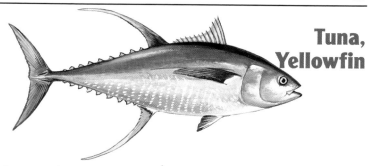

Tuna, Yellowfin

Yellowfin are caught more frequently in New Jersey waters than any other tuna except for false albacore. They range in size from a few pounds to nearly 300, and they feed at the surface and well down in the water column. They often appear in schools; consequently anglers hooking one yellowfin should brace for more action from schoolmates.

DESCRIPTION: Yellowfins are beautiful and colorful tuna, with dark blue or black back and yellow on the sides, with fins tinged in yellow and yellow finlets. Silvery gold on the flanks, yellowfins are silvery white below. The clearest identifying characteristic of the yellowfin – found in larger specimens – are extremely long second dorsal and anal fins. However, many of their physical characteristics are shared with others, including dark back fading to light undersides and yellow finlets trimmed in black.

WHERE AND WHEN: As with other tuna species, the deep waters of the far offshore canyons are prime hunting grounds for yellowfins. The nutrient rich Gulf Stream water brings concentrations of bait up to the NJ canyons every year and the tuna along with it. As noted, the Hudson Canyon is a prime hunting ground for big game anglers, but the other five canyons south of the Hudson – Carteret, Toms, Spencer, Lindenkohl and Wilmington Canyons – all can be exceptionally productive as well.

BAIT AND TACKLE: The general rule of thumb is daytime trolling in the early season and daytime trolling and nighttime chunking later in the season. Trolling both rigged natural baits such as ballyhoos and sardines and an array of large artificials can produce strikes. Anglers often chunk fish at night from boats tied to buoys, working in a chunk slick of butter fish or menhaden. Lights in the water at night attract bait, prominently to include squid. (Note: in general the best bait for tuna is live squid, so anglers should try to snag or net as many as possible as they swim up to the lights.) Since yellowfins can run to substantial size, it is prudent to work bait or lures on strong stand up tackle.

STATE RECORD: The state record yellowfin tuna was caught by builder Wayne Brinkerhoff when fishing in the Wilmington Canyon in 1980 The tuna weighed 290 pounds.

FOOD VALUE: The yellowfin is one of the best tasting of the tunas, whether cooked lightly or served raw in sashimi. ■

Tuna, Little Tunny / False Albacore

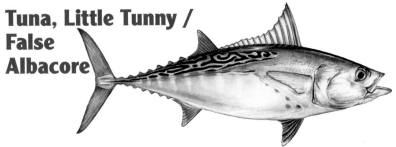

The little tunny, also known as false albacore, is the most common tuna in the Atlantic Ocean, and certainly one of its finest small game fish. Swimming at speeds of 40 m.p.h., the little tunny maximizes its compact, streamlined body to facilitate long runs and endurance that is remarkable for a fish its size.

DESCRIPTION: The little tunny's markings make it easy to distinguish from similar species like the skipjack tuna and Atlantic bonito. Its scattering of dark, fingerprint-like spots between the pectoral and pelvic fins cannot be found on any related Atlantic species.

WHERE AND WHEN: The little tunny's preferred habitat often is much closer to shore than most other tunas, often in schools. They relate to inlets, points, jetties and sandbars — all haunts where bait fish like menhaden form large schools. However, little tunny avoid the brackish water of estuaries. They also are found offshore in deeper water, competing for forage fish with bluefish and bonito. The prime season is the fall.

BAIT AND TACKLE: Prepare to fight a false albacore with strong tackle with the knowledge that a 10 pound fish will snap 20 pound test line in a heartbeat. It is often possible to approach a school of little tunny to cast jigs, small plugs and lures. Indeed, sight casting with lures like Swedish Pimples, Crippled Herring, Tormentors and Tsunamis is thought to be the most exciting way to catch these muscular fish.

Trollers catch them on everything from live bait to offshore lures. Little tunny also are caught from anchored and drifting boats, often on chunk baits.

STATE RECORD: Mark Niemczyk was fishing off Sea Bright when he caught his state record 24 pound 15 ounce "Albie" in 1997.

FOOD VALUE: Although consumed in other cultures, the little tunny, with its reddish purple flesh, is not highly prized as table fare in New Jersey. However, the oily, blood-filled flesh is a fine bait when cut in strips or skinned and used by trollers who value the bright flash to attract fish. ■

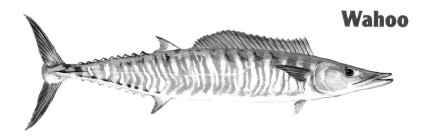

Wahoo

The wahoo is quite possibly the fastest swimmer among all game fish, reportedly reaching speeds of 68 m.p.h. It is especially known for the speed and strength of its first run, melting 150 yards of line off a reel in a blink and burning out the drags of some reels. It is a highly prized and exciting quarry, especially when taken on light to medium tackle.

DESCRIPTION: The wahoo is a torpedo-shaped fish with an iridescent blue back and silvery sides marked with a pattern of irregular vertical blue bars. The mouth is large and both the upper and lower jaws are armed with razor sharp teeth. Although normally much smaller, the wahoo can grow to six feet in length and more than 120 pounds in weight.

WHERE AND WHEN: Wahoo, like tuna, are usually caught in the deep offshore waters of the Spencer, Lindenkohl, Carteret and Hudson Canyons. Mid-summer is prime time for wahoos, which most often are a surprise by-catch for anglers trolling rigged ballyhoo in search of tuna or marlin.

BAIT AND TACKLE: Most wahoo are taken on excessively heavy tackle by anglers questing after much larger sportfish. It is thought that 99% of wahoo caught in New Jersey waters are accidentally picked up by anglers working heavy boat tackle. While a full spool of line with 30 pound test line would be sufficient, most wahoos fall to 100 pound test line or better

since the intended target out in the canyons is tuna.

STATE RECORD: The state record wahoo was a surprise in several respects. First, while they generally run considerably smaller, Robert Carr caught a record fish weighing 123 pounds 12 ounces. Second, while "hoos" are normally found in deep blue water much further offshore, Robert caught his beast at the 28-mile wreck in South Jersey.

FOOD VALUE: Because the wahoo is such a spectacular game fish, it should be released alive whenever possible. However, when this is not possible, there may not be a better tasting fish in the sea than wahoo. The meat is incredibly white and the texture suits it perfectly to be eaten as sashimi, sushi or very lightly seared. ▪

Weakfish

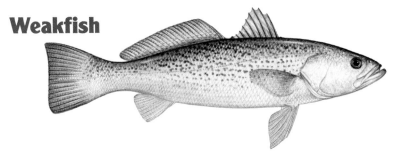

The weakfish is so named because of its fragile mouth structure, in which weak muscles allow hooks to tear away quite easily. In fact, weakfish are not otherwise weak at all. They are powerful swimmers and first rate fighters. Members of the drum family, weakfish are also known as gray sea trout. At one time they schooled in the thousands in our coastal waters, but commercial and recreational fishing have diminished their numbers. They are making a comeback but may never reappear in the huge schools that once existed.

DESCRIPTION: Weakfish are among our most beautiful and colorful species. They are bright silver with small spots throughout their bodies and yellowish unmarked fins. They are easily differentiated from spotted sea trout, which are marked with black spots throughout their bodies as well as on their dorsal fins. The average sized weakfish caught in our rivers and bays range from one to three pounds, with a few as large as 10 pounds.

WHERE AND WHEN: Weakies usually arrive in our coastal waters in early summer and stay until mid September. Larger fish caught in the spring are usually breeders and should be released in the interest of conservation. Delaware Bay is perhaps the most popular weakfishing area in the country, and the mouth of the Mullica River and Meyers Hole in Barnegat Bay are also popular destinations. "Schoolie" sized fish are found in numbers off the beach in summer, at which time drifting boats using strip baits score well.

BAIT AND TACKLE: Although weaks are good fighters, saltwater spinning gear or a quality bait casting outfit is more than sufficiently heavy for the task. Sandworms on long-leadered gold bait-holder hooks in size 2/0 will do the trick when fishing river mouths and bays. Offshore a two hook rig on two foot leaders – one five feet above the sinker and the other tied in at the sinker dropper loop – will catch schoolies, especially when baited with a long thin strip of fresh cut squid, hooked once. Shedder crab pieces also work well.

STATE RECORD: Karl Jones caught his record 18 pound 6 ounce weakfish in 1986 in Delaware Bay. (The record spotted sea trout, a rarity in New Jersey waters, was caught in the surf in Holgate by Bert Harper in 1974. It weighed 11 pounds 2 ounces.)

FOOD VALUE: The flesh of the weakfish is white, sweet, lean and finely textured. It makes a delicious meal when fried, broiled or cooked whole with stuffing in the oven or on the grill. ■

About The Authors

Manny Luftglass and Ron Bern have been friends and fishing buddies for 40 years, during which time they have spent thousands of hours together fishing the richest and most productive fresh and saltwater venues throughout New Jersey. Many of their conversations between strikes have centered on the fish they sought: species of fish, where and when to catch them, best baits and tackle, most effective presentation of lures and flies and bait, record sizes, and although both practice catch and release almost exclusively, even the table worthiness of one species versus another.

Manny and Ron shared their extensive knowledge of the best and most productive fishing venues in their widely read book, *Gone Fishin': The 100 Best Spots in New Jersey,* originally published by Rutgers University Press. Now they are sharing their in-depth insights into the fish they avidly seek in *Sport Fish of New Jersey: An Angler's Guide.*

Both authors bring a great deal of experience to the telling. Manny is the author of twelve successful books on fishing. In his "Gone

Fishin'" series, he authored books titled: *The 50 Best Waters in Pennsylvania, Florida's 100 Best Salt Waters, Massachusetts' 100 Best Waters, The 75 Best Waters in Connecticut* and *Fishing for Beginners.* In addition, he has authored books about fishing in Lake Hopatcong, Round Valley Reservoir, Spruce Run Reservoir and New Jersey Saltwater Rivers and Bays and species-specific books on fishing for hybrid bass and carp. He co-authored *Gone Fishin': The 100 Best Spots in New York* with Ron Bern, also published by Rutgers University Press, and *Gone Fishin' With Kids* with Joe Perrone, Jr. He is a frequent contributor to major outdoor publications and is a book publisher under the name Gone Fishin' Enterprises. He was the mayor of Somerville, NJ.

Ron Bern is the author of eight published books, including two novels, *The Legacy* and *Mule Maddox,* and non-fiction books on business subjects, in addition to three co-authored books on fishing. He is a career writer and editor and for many years was president of a management consulting firm in New York. He is a member of "Who's Who" in America.

INDEX

28-mile wreck 83

A

Aeroflex Lake 2

Alfaiate, Fernando (record king mackerel) 58

Assunpink Lake 21

Atlantic City Jetty 73

Avogardo, Eric (record rock bass) 12

B

Barnegat Bay 52, 55, 84

Barnegat Light 53, 54

Bass River 62

Bear Swamp Creek 4

Belsky, Robert Jr. (record spot) 72

Benchley, Peter ("Jaws") 67

Bests Pond 11

Big Flatbrook River 5, 7

Black Brook Park Pond 16

Black River 1

blue nose perch 62

Boonton Reservoir 20

Brielle 44, 63

Brinkerhoff, Wayne
(record yellowfin tuna) 81

Brown, Frederick
(Atlantic croaker record) 45

Budd Lake 20, 26

C

Cape May 28, 39, 40, 47, 52, 55, 58, 59, 80

Cape May Point 72

Cape Shore Channel 72

Carnegie Lake 29

Carr, Robert (record wahoo) 83

Carteret Canyon 81, 83

Chanda, Dave v, x

Cherokee bass 32

Chesla, Joseph (codrish record) 44

Christian, John
(freshwater record striped bass) 73

Cohansey River 1

Cranberry Lake 27, 28, 29, 32

Crow Shoal 72

Culver Lake 32

Cunner 46

Curlis Lake 18

D

Dallenbach Pond 20

Deal 30

Deal Lake 66

Delaware Bay 45, 49, 52, 64, 72, 73, 84

Delaware River 9, 13, 15, 19, 20, 25, 26, 31, 35

Demsey, Jack Jr. (record grass carp) 18